Soon *and*
Very Soon

Soon *and*
Very Soon

A Biblical and Theological Study
of the Events Surrounding
Jesus Christ's Second Coming

David K. Hebert, ThD

WORD & SPIRIT PRESS
Tulsa, Oklahoma

Soon and Very Soon: A Biblical and Theological Study of the Events Surrounding Jesus Christ's Second Coming

Copyright © 2019 by David K. Hebert.

Lyrics to Michael Blanchard, "Be Ye Glad,"1980 Newspring Publishing Inc. (ASCAP; adm. at Capitol CMG Publishing), are used by permission.

Published by Word & Spirit Press LLC, Tulsa, OK

Cover design by BookSetters

Composed at Pressbooks.com using the Clarke design, by Angela Sample

ISBN: 978-1-943489-03-9 (softcover)

ISBN: 978-1-943489-04-6 (ebook)

Printed in the United States of America

Contents

Preface

I got saved in the fall of 1974 at the United States Coast Guard Academy in New London, Connecticut, alone in my barracks room after hearing a lecture on "David's Five Smooth Stones" by Christian author Patricia O. Brooks (mother of one of my classmates—John Brooks). Right afterwards, I got interested in what is known in the Christian vernacular as the "End Times" or "Last Days." I was told, like every other young Christian at the start of one's discipleship journey, to read the Book of John first, which I did. And then, I read the entire New Testament three times, probably in a month. Of course that means that three times I came upon the Book of Revelation. And what does one do with Revelation? So at that time (in the 1970s, during the Jesus Movement and the Charismatic Movement), when the Dispensational Movement was in full swing also, the End Times was being taught coincidentally with the ongoing revival. And in my case, the biggest part of understanding the End Times, or the terminology of the events surrounding the Second Coming of the Lord Jesus Christ, appeared to be the Rapture. So this begged the question, "What is the Rapture?"

That question is really what started everything with me. As a result, I set out to answer that one particular question in my mind. Now, you have to understand that this was back before all the Christian personality tests, spiritual gifts tests, and things like that (and even personal computers and the Internet). What I did not understand at the time was this interest and passion was a large part of what God uniquely created me to be—my God-given gift of teaching and researching about the End-Times and Satan's End-Times' deceptive "false gospel."

That began my research into the Rapture, and everything surrounding it. I began to understand that this was not just a New Testament thing, but that it was fundamentally based on concepts addressed in the Old Testament (not the least of which were the "raptures" of Enoch in G en 5:23–24 and Elijah in 2 Kgs 2:1–12). As time went on, and I gained more knowledge and understanding of all of these concepts, the next thing in my mind was to be able to communicate these concepts to other Christians. So, I started to develop a Bible Study on the End Times, which was expanded and edited over the next twenty-five years or so (during twenty of which I served in the Coast Guard: 1978–1998), with help from many of the laypeople involved in those studies. Eventually, I completed a master's degree in Theological & Historical Studies from Oral Roberts University (ORU) in 2006.

However, before that, and upon entering the program in 2004, I knew that I would write my master's thesis on the Rapture of the Church. And as a confirmation of this in my life and a testimony to the urgency of the task, Oral Roberts received a vision from the Lord in August of 2004. In this vision, he was shown that neither the Church nor the world was ready for the Second Coming of the Lord Jesus Christ. The Second Coming would be separated into two parts: 1) the Rapture of the Church in the clouds; and 2) the return of the Lord Jesus the second time to earth to judge the nations (at Armageddon). Also, the Church had not been fully doing its job by proclaiming the Second Coming in conjunction with preaching and teaching the Gospel of Jesus Christ.

After completing the master's work, I completed my doctoral degree from the University of South Africa (UNISA) in May 2010. The doctoral work was an offshoot of the master's thesis on the Rapture of the Church, and involved melding both comings of Jesus into the understanding of the Perfect/

Complete Gospel compared to the false gospel of Satan. Finally in the summer of 2010, I was able to teach a master's level class at ORU on Biblical Eschatology (based on all the work I'd done over the years for the Bible studies, the master's thesis, and the doctoral work). All along in my mind, I was thinking that my research and writing would finally answer the question I first asked at the beginning of my salvation: What is the Rapture? And, I believe that it did!

The Lord confirmed this for me on the southernmost tip of the African Continent in May 2010, at Cape Agulhas, South Africa, where two oceans (Indian and Atlantic) become one, by providing a special experience viewed by my wife, our tour-guide friend (Tommy O' Kennedy), and me (along with about five-to-ten other tourists). We saw a double rainbow (one atop the other, as a mirror-reflection), followed by a single rainbow, both arching over Cape Agulhas and touching one side on the Indian Ocean and the other side on the Atlantic Ocean.

The initial indication and understanding of this experience was, "two becoming one." Although this understanding could be applied to many subjects, on many levels, I believe that it confirmed my understanding that the Perfect/Complete Gospel involves both comings of Jesus Christ being melded into one. And, that the beginning of the events surrounding the Second Coming of Jesus would be the Rapture of the Church.

Therefore, it is my sincere hope and belief that this book will help to answer the initial question of the Rapture, and all other related "End-Times" questions, for all believers: both new and old, student and layperson alike. I also believe that this book is timely and for this generation, especially considering the times in which we live—in these Last Days of New World Order, New Age, Post-Modernism, Relativism, Radical Islamic Terrorism, and increased natural and human-made disasters, where truth seems to be individually relative, deceptive heresy is taught as truth, the love of many has grown cold, and many people are lovers of self and pleasure rather than lovers of God (Matt 24:12; 1 Tim 4:1; 2 Tim 3:1–7; Jude 17–19). This culture has not taken place in a vacuum, but in an exponentially increasing explosion of knowledge, communication, and transportation, foretold by Daniel the Prophet some 2,500 years ago (Dan 12:4). And, most of this has occurred since the rebirth of Israel as a nation on May 14, 1948, which is itself a fulfillment of eschatological prophecy (Isa 66:7–9; Ezek 37:15–28; Amos 9:15). Therefore, I also hope and pray that this book will encourage those who read it and invite each reader to share its contents with as many believers and unbelievers in one's sphere of influence. And until that day and hour of the "Blessed Hope" of the Rapture of the Church, let our heart's cry be the same as the Early Church's: Maranatha!—Lord Jesus, Come!

June 2019

1.

Introduction

What Do People Think of When They Hear "End Times," "Last Days," "End of the Age," "Revelation," or "The Apocalypse"?

End of the world? Armageddon? Judgment? The Second Coming of Jesus Christ? The Rapture of the Church and who will be a part of it? Are we living in the End Times? Or, all of the above? Many Christians try to read the Book of Revelation for answers to these and other questions, and end up asking themselves, "What does all this mean?" Or, "What does this mean *to me*?" and "*When* will all this happen?"

However, don't be dismayed, disheartened, or discouraged—be encouraged! If this is how you feel, then you are in good company. The disciples asked Jesus the same type of questions on two separate occasions: 1) during the Apocalyptic (Olivet) Discourse (recorded in Matt 24:3; Mark 13:4; Luke 21:7); and 2) just before Jesus' Ascension (recorded in Acts 1:6).[1] So you see, these types of questions regarding "the end of all things" are very common, and are an innate part of human existence, especially, when one is in relationship with the Alpha and Omega, the Beginning and the End, the Author and Finisher, Perfecter and Completer, of all creation—the Triune God of the Bible (Isa 41:4; Heb 12:2; Rev 1:8).

When considering the End Times or Last Days, a plethora of terms and related questions come to the forefront, including the following: End of the World, New World Order, wars/rumors of wars, earthquakes, famines, Armageddon, the Antichrist, the mark of the Beast, 666, plagues, the wrath of God, the Great Tribulation, the Second Coming (Advent) or Return of Jesus Christ, the Rapture of the Church, the Millennium, the Judgment Seat of Christ, the Marriage Supper of the Lamb, and others. As you can see, there is much to be considered when addressing this topic.

But when specifically asked if they have read the Book of Revelation (and the corresponding prophetic portions of the Book of Daniel), most Christians answer that they feel too intimidated to even begin to read or study the passages. And if some have taken that first courageous step and read the entire material through, most come away from the experience asking more questions than when they started. However, if you would happen upon a good, simple, and straightforward book, commentary, or teacher to help guide you through this process (such as, *The Book of Revelation Revealed*, by Hilton Sutton), you would begin to understand the promise of the blessing contained in Revelation 1:3: *"Blessed is he who reads and those who hear the words of the prophecy, and heed the things which are written in it* [emphasis added]; for the time is near."

Thus, this book is dedicated to all Christians who have these burning questions in their hearts and minds, especially as we look at the current events happening in not only the Middle East, but around the world today. This book's secondary purpose is to expose the deception of Satan's End-Times, deceptive, false religious cults that are so pervasive in the current day and age. Therefore, we join with Paul (in 1 Cor 16:22), John and Jesus (in Rev 22:20), and the Early Church every time they celebrated Holy Communion in exclaiming: *Maranatha*—Lord Jesus, come![2]

I have maintained an avid interest in the issues surrounding the

End Times for about thirty-five years, and this study should help to address most, if not all, of the above questions or areas of interest. This book is prepared as a guide to Biblical Eschatology (study of the End-Times'/Last Days' events surrounding the Second Coming of the Lord Jesus Christ),[3] and has been put into a chapter-by-chapter, concept-by-concept format. However at this point, there needs to be a couple of recommendations given. I was discipled, or "trained-up in the Lord," in the middle of the Jesus Movement (in the 1970s) in a charismatic, yet evangelical and Bible-based environment. I was taught to read and study the Bible voraciously with the help of the Holy Spirit and prayer (as if it were truly the milk, bread, and meat necessary to sustain the soul—1 Pet 2:2–3). And furthermore, when being taught by a Bible teacher who quoted various scripture verses, I was also encouraged to *check each and every verse for myself,* to ensure its proper veracity and usage in context. Thus, my advice to you as the reader of this book is to do the same—*check each scripture cited for yourself.* In doing so, I believe that you will be truly blessed and receive a fuller, deeper understanding of these End Times concepts. Also, as you may have already noticed, end notes have been provided for the readers who would like to check the source(s) of the cited information for further information.

At this point one might ask, "Why another book about End-times?" or "How is this different from other books about the End-Times?" Aside from the fact that this is my passion (and I would go so far as to say that this is what God uniquely created me to do), I believe the answer to these questions lies in the form of another question: *"When* is one's salvation complete?" Although this appears to be a re-opening of the debate on "Once Saved, Always Saved," eternal security, predestination, or Calvinism versus Arminianism, it is not!

The Early Church believers understood the answer to this

question at the moment they made the choice to follow Jesus of Nazareth as their Messiah, Savior, and Lord. Because at that time, this was a matter of life and death—there was a very real possibility that a new Christian could be martyred for his or her faith at any time in that first-century AD world. So, what was this "Blessed Hope" (Titus 2:13) that the early Christians longed for? The answer is contained in the last small phrase of the Apostle's Creed: "…the resurrection of the body, and the life everlasting. AMEN."[4] Traditionally, the Apostle's Creed, or some similar confession of faith, accompanied the prayer of salvation and baptism at each Christian's salvation in the Early Church. Therefore, the answer to the question of when or what constitutes the completion of a Christian's salvation is: *at the resurrection of the body*!

This then begs the follow-up question, "*When* does the resurrection of the body take place?" Again, the Early Church believers understood that the resurrection of the body was inseparably connected to the Second Coming of the Lord Jesus Christ. So, the short answer to the question is: the completion of each Christian's salvation occurs as part of the Second Coming of Jesus! All of this to say, salvation made possible by Jesus' First Coming is completed for the entire, universal Body of Christ at Jesus' Second Coming. The revelation of this idea in this day and age has helped me to identify this concept as the Perfect/Complete Gospel of Both Comings of Jesus Christ. And, therein remains the culminating motivation to write this book.

I believe that the Perfect/Complete Gospel of Both Comings of Jesus Christ is best encapsulated by Paul in Philippians 1:6 (New Living Translation NLT): "*And I am sure that God, who began the good work within you will continue his work until it is finally finished on that day when Christ Jesus comes back again* [emphasis added]." In this one verse, the entirety of the good news (Gospel) of salvation is broken down: a) "God, who began the good work"—*justification*/new creation of the Christian in Christ Jesus (Rom 3:20–30; 2 Cor 5:14b–18a); b) "will continue His work"—*sanctification* (becoming Christ-like) process of the Holy Spirit (Rom 8:1–17; 12:1–2; Gal 5:22–23); c) "until it is finished"—*glorification*, when Christians receive their new spiritual bodies like Jesus did at His resurrection (Rom 8:18–25; 1 Cor 15:20–24; 50–55; 1 Thess 4:14–18). Therefore as in a marriage, where "two become one" (Matt 19:4–6), this Perfect/Complete Gospel concept cohesively unifies Jesus' First Coming (for redemption, reconciliation, and restoration) with His Second Coming (for the Rapture and Resurrection of the Body of Christ) into the complete salvation of the Body of Christ (both corporately and individually). This is also addressed by the prayer of thanksgiving (or declaration of the "Mystery of the Faith"): "Christ has died, Christ has risen, and Christ will come again."[5]

If this is not enough justification for a book such as this, consider the eschatological vision Oral Roberts received from God in the late summer of 2004. This occurred right as I was entering into my master's study of theology at Oral Roberts University. It became a personal confirmation and motivation from God for me to continue my studies in this arena, and to "get this information out" to the Body of Christ at large. In this vision, Oral Roberts was shown that neither the present-day Church nor the world is ready for the Second Coming of the Lord Jesus Christ. Thus, the Church has not been fully doing its job by proclaiming the Second Coming in conjunction with preaching the Gospel of the Lord Jesus.[6] This experience planted the seed of the concept of the Perfect/Complete Gospel in my heart, and came to fruition with the completion of my doctoral work in 2010: "The Need for Teaching the Eschatological Gospel of Both Comings of Jesus Christ in the

Twenty-First Century, Especially as We See the Day of His *Parousia* Approaching."[7]

The Church, especially the Western Church, appears to be living in the Laodicean Period (Rev 3:14–20) of the Church Age (the time between Jesus' First Coming and Second Coming). According to the scholars listed in the end note at the end of this sentence, this Laodicean Period is the last period of the Church Age just prior to the Rapture of the Church (symbolized by the individual rapture of Jesus Himself in Acts 1:6–11 and Rev 12:5).[8] This End-Time Church appears to fulfill the Laodicean description contained in the Book of Revelation as follows: looking inward versus outward; being rich, self-sufficient, and complacent; and becoming lethargic and lukewarm by allowing Secular Humanism, moral compromise, and the social gospel to infiltrate its own body (the very Body of Christ), while actually being wretched and miserable, and poor, blind, and naked (Rev 3:17). The answer to this plight is found in the following verses of Revelation 3:18–20, in the form of an invitation by Jesus:

> I advise you to buy from Me gold refined by the fire, that you may become rich, and white garments, that you may clothe yourself, and that the shame of your nakedness may not be revealed; and eyesalve to anoint your eyes, that you may see. Those whom I love, I reprove and discipline; be zealous therefore, and repent. *Behold, I stand at the door and knock; if anyone hears My voice and opens the door, I will come in to him, and will dine with him, and he with Me* [emphasis added].

This solution is also mentioned in Revelation 1:1–3 and 19:10: "The Revelation of Jesus Christ, which God gave Him to show His bond-servants, the things which must shortly take place…. Blessed is he who reads and those who hear the words of the prophecy, and heed the things which are written in it; *for the time is near…worship God. For the testimony of Jesus is the spirit of prophecy"* [emphasis added]—the Perfect/Complete Gospel!

Additionally, let us look at the "other side of the coin"—Satan's false gospel. In these days of New World Order, New Age, Post-Modernism, Relativism, and the meteoric rise of Radical Islam as a world religion, truth seems to be individually relative, deceptive heresy is taught as truth, the love of many has grown cold, and most people are lovers of self and pleasure rather than lovers of God (Matt 24:12; 1 Tim 4:1; 2 Tim 3:1–7; Jude 17–19). Or, as famous recording artist Noel Paul Stookey (from the group "Peter, Paul, and Mary") sang in the 1980 song "Be Ye Glad" (written by Michael Blanchard):

> And in these days of confused situations;
>
> And in these nights of a restless remorse;
>
> When the heart and the soul of a nation lay wounded and cold as a corpse.
>
> From the grave of the innocent Adam comes a song bringing joy to the sad.
>
> All your cries have been heard and the ransom has been paid up in full,
>
> Be ye glad...[9]

This culture has not taken place in a vacuum, but in an exponentially increasing explosion of knowledge, communication, and transportation, as foretold by the Prophet Daniel some 2,500 years ago (Dan 12:4). However, most of this has primarily occurred in the short timeframe since the rebirth of the Nation of Israel on May 14, 1948,[10] which in and of itself is a fulfillment of eschatological biblical prophecy (Isa 66:7–9; Ezek 37:15–28; Amos 9:15). Yet, this new global experience still gives evidence of humanity's innate interest in its spiritual nature, which was born, and then died (with the Original Sin/ Fall of Humanity), in the Garden of Eden (Gen 2–3) around 6,000 years ago.[11] Yet, humanity is still longing to be in right relationship with its Creator as originally designed (Gen 1:26 – 2:25). And, there is "faith, hope, and love, and the greatest of these is love" (1 Cor 13:13), to allow each person to reconcile that relationship with God (2 Cor 5:19)!

Therefore today, there remains a critical and very-present need for discerning truth from error, Christian orthodoxy from heresy, and the Perfect/Complete Gospel of the Kingdom of God from the false gospel of the kingdom of Satan. This may be contextualized by the Parable of the Wheat and Weeds (Matt 13:24–30, 36–43). In this parable, Jesus talks about both the Kingdom of God and the kingdom of darkness coexisting and growing unhindered, side-by-side, until the "end of the age." This typifies that in every generation since the Fall of Adam and Eve in the Garden of Eden (Gen 3), God has placed the opportunity to choose to be in relationship with Him (Kingdom of God), or to choose to believe Satan's lie (to be like God—Gen 3:5), and go one's own way (kingdom of darkness).

With that as a general introduction, let us delve a bit more specifically (biblically and theologically) into this concept of the Perfect/Complete Gospel of Both Comings of Jesus Christ, as a solid foundation for this entire study. This Perfect/Complete Gospel concept was intimated and patterned in the Old Testament by the Creation Week (Gen 1:1–2:3, including the concept of seventh-day rest—Sabbath), promise, deliverance, covenant, law, and Kingship Theology.[12] These concepts were confirmed through the Old Testament offices of prophet, priest, and king, Israel's Feasts or Festivals (Lev 23), and Theophanies or Christophanies (appearances of God; e.g., Gen 18; Gen 32:22–32; Exod 3; Josh 5:13–15). And finally, this concept was foretold by Old Testament prophets through various Kingdom of God and First and Second Coming of Messiah prophecies (e.g., Isa 9:6–7; 11:11–12; 61:1–11; Dan 2; 7:13–14; and 9; Micah 5:2–15).[13] These concepts will be developed more in the chapters to come.

This Perfect/Complete Gospel was initiated by Jesus Himself and taught to His disciples nearly two thousand years ago via direct teaching (i.e., Matt 24; Mark 13; Luke 17:20–37; 21; John 14:1–28); the parables about the Kingdom of God (e.g., Matt 13); the Lord's Prayer (Luke 11:1–4); the Words of Institution at the Last Supper (Matt 26:26–29; 1 Cor 11:23–26); and the Great Commission (Matt 28:18–20).[14] After Jesus' death, burial, resurrection, and ascension, James, Paul, Peter, the writer of Hebrews, Jude, and John[15] then taught Jesus' Perfect/Complete Gospel to the Christian Church.[16] A good way of describing the totality and importance of the role of Scripture in addressing the Perfect/Complete Gospel is put forth in an article in *Christianity Today* entitled "The Gospel of the Blessed Hope":

> The *preaching and writings of the Old Testament prophets focused always upon the promised* **incarnation of God in Jesus Christ** *as the event in history that would give purpose to their utterances.* So also the *proclamations of the New Testament preachers and writers point ever to* **the second coming of Jesus Christ** *at the culmination of history as that "one far-off divine event, to which the whole creation moves"* [emphasis added]. There is no book or message in the New Testament which does not expressly declare or imply the return of our Lord as that "blessed hope" of those whose trust is fixed in him.[17]

However in theological terms, the Perfect/Complete Gospel is based on the combination of two theological concepts: eschatology and gospel. The word eschatology derives from the Greek word *eschatos*, meaning "the extreme, most remote spoken of place and time, the last," the study of last things, End Times, or final events surrounding the Second Coming (*Parousia*) of the Lord Jesus Christ.[18] This concept is further refined, and *probably more appropriately communicated*, by understanding the meaning of the Greek words *telos* or *teleios* as, "fulfillment, completion, perfection, goal, whole, full, entire, or *perfect, complete* [emphasis added]."[19]

The word gospel is understood from two Greek words—*euangelion*, meaning "a good message, good news, the Gospel of Jesus Christ,"[20] and *martyreo/martyria*, meaning "to witness/a witness,"—taken together to mean, the "good news" or witness about Jesus Christ coming to redeem and restore humanity back from sin into right relationship with God.[21] From this understanding and combination of these two theological concepts of eschatology/teleiology and gospel comes the theological idea of the *Perfect/Complete Gospel*. We now press on to a discussion of Christian orthodoxy versus heresy, in light of the Parable of Wheat and Weeds in Matthew 13.

The early beginnings of Christian orthodoxy date back prior to the Early Church's confessions or creeds, to the Old Testament Mosaic Covenant God made with the Israelites (e.g., the Ten Commandments of Exod 20:1–17; the confession of God's attributes by Moses at Mt. Horeb [Sinai] in Exod 34:6–7; and the *Shema* ["Hear O Israel"] of Deut 6:4–9). The Early Church then accepted the entire Old Testament as Holy Scripture at the Synod of Jamnia (AD 70–100).[22] As mentioned earlier, the Early Church's confessions or creeds were normally spoken at conversion or upon baptism of the Christian. The most simple of these was "Jesus is Lord" (Rom 10:9–10, 1 Cor 12:3, and the expanded version of Phil 2:6–11). There was also the Gospel encapsulated in 1 Corinthians 15:3–8 and what has become known as the Apostles' Creed (later expanded by the Nicene and Athanasian Creeds).[23] Additionally, the "Rule of Faith or Truth" was attested to by Early Church Fathers Irenaeus, Tertullian, Origen, and Athanasius as revealed truth reflected in the baptismal confession, the Scriptures, and the preaching of the Church.[24]

Therefore, the Christian view of orthodoxy was founded on the teachings of Jesus and the tradition of the Apostolic Church.[25] And finally, the basis and ultimate authority for all Christian orthodoxy became the complete New Testament Scriptures, which were officially closed at the Council of Carthage (AD 397).[26] From this firm foundation, came the other two means of determining Christian orthodoxy: tradition (historic faith of the Church) and reason (based on a tension between faith or spirituality and reason).[27] To simplify, the *central (core) orthodox doctrines* of the Christian faith are synthesized as follows:

> ...*the Trinity* [Triune God of the Bible—the Father, the Son, the Holy Spirit], *the deity of Christ, the bodily resurrection* [Jesus was the first], *the atoning work of Christ on the cross, and salvation by grace through faith* [emphasis added]. These doctrines so comprise the essence of the Christian faith that to remove any of them is to make the belief system non-Christian…. All Christian denominations—whether Roman Catholic, Eastern Orthodox, or Protestant—agree on the essential core.[28]

The term "orthodoxy" comes from the following two Greek words: *orthos*, literally meaning, "right, rising, perpendicular (erect), or horizontal (level/direct)," which came to mean straight or upright;[29] and *dokeo*, meaning, "to believe, to think, to have the appearance, or to count for something."[30] Therefore, the term orthodoxy could be defined as, "correct or sound belief according to an authoritative norm"; and heterodoxy as, "belief in a doctrine differing from the norm."[31] This "norm" in our case is the core orthodox doctrines of the Christian faith mentioned above. On the other hand, the term "heresy" has come to mean an erroneous teaching, a sect with erroneous (or false) beliefs,[32] or *a teaching that subverts the central Christian doctrines.*[33]

Now with a firm understanding of the concepts of the Perfect/Complete Gospel of Both Comings of Jesus Christ and Christian orthodoxy versus heresy, within the framework of the Parable of the Wheat and Weeds, in the next chapters, let us press forward with the examination of the following subjects with the Holy Spirit as our guide into all truth (John 16:13–15):

- Prophecy and Interpretation of Prophecy
- Time (*Kairos* Time, *Chronos* Time, Biblical Time, and Salvation History) and Biblical Timelines
- The Kingdom of Heaven—God and Biblical Covenants
- The Second Coming of Jesus Christ (*Parousia*)
- The Millennium
- The Day of the LORD (*Yahweh*)
- The Rapture of the Church
- Intermediate State, Eternal State , and Associated Resurrections and Judgments
- The Signs of the Times

2.

Defining Biblical Prophecy
What It Is and How to Interpret It

Before a discussion about biblical prophecy and its interpretation can begin, we must first consider the broader questions about the Bible's revelation, inspiration, infallibility, and inerrancy. In regards to the Bible's revelation and inspiration, there are two primary passages that describe not only the Bible in general, but biblical prophecy specifically: 2 Tim 3:16, "All Scripture is *God-breathed* and is useful for…"; and 2 Pet 1:19–21, "…no prophecy was ever made by an act of human will, *but men moved by the Holy Spirit spoke from God*" [emphasis added]. These two seminal passages are confirmed by others regarding the inspiration of both the Old Testament (e.g., Deut 18:18; 2 Sam 23:2; Isa 59:21; Zech 7:12) and the New Testament (1 Cor 2:13; 14:37; 1 Tim 5:18; 2 Pet 3:15–16; Rev 1:1; 22:9).[1] As Hebrews 4:12 asserts, the Bible is often referred to as the "Word of God." Thus, we may understand that the Word of God is inspired not only verbally ("located in the words"), but also in the plenary sense ("it extends to every part of the words and all they teach or imply").[2] With this as a foundational understanding of the revelation and inspiration of the Bible, we may further conclude that "the Bible is thereby the infallible rule and final authority for faith and practice for all believers."[3] The discussion now turns to an understanding of infallibility and inerrancy.

Infallibility may be defined as, "what has divine authority; what cannot be broken (John 10:34–35)." Correspondingly, inerrancy may be defined as, "what is without error; wholly true."[4] The biblical basis for infallibility/inerrancy comes from the previous discussion on inspiration: that the Bible is "God-breathed" (2 Tim 3:16); that it claims to have divine authority, which is above all human authority (Matt 5:17–18; 15:3–6); and that it is called the Word of God (2 Chr 34:14; Zech 7:12; John 10:35; Heb 4:12). Additionally, there remains the claim that since God is truth (John 14:6) and cannot err or lie (Titus 1:2; Heb 6:18), then the Word of God cannot err (Ps 119:160; John 17:17; Rom 3:4).[5] Therefore, this brief discussion on biblical infallibility and inerrancy confirms the above statement: *The Bible is the divine, infallible, and inerrant rule and authority for all believers in all matters of faith, practice, and ultimately, life.* At this point, however, a brief discussion about the difference between the Catholic and Protestant Bibles needs to be addressed.

As mentioned in Chapter 1, the entire thirty-nine books of the Old Testament were accepted by the Early Church as Holy Scripture at the Synod of Jamnia (AD 70–100).[6] Both the Catholic and Protestant Churches agree on this. In fact, both churches also accept the entire twenty-seven books of the New Testament (when the entire Canon, or standard, of the Bible was officially closed at the Council of Carthage, AD 397).[7] The difference of opinion comes some 1,150 years later from the Council of Trent (1546), which was the Roman Catholic response to the Protestant Reformation initiated by Martin Luther's Ninety-five Theses (1517). At the Council of Trent, eleven or twelve (if Baruch 1–6 is split into two books—Baruch 1–5 and Baruch 6) books were added to the Catholic Bible. These books are called *The Apocrypha* by Protestants and Jews, and Deutero-Canonical (Second Canon) by the Catholics.[8] Although this difference in Protestant and Catholic Bibles still remains today, I believe that one must apply the same standards and scrutiny mentioned above regarding inspiration and inerrancy that the Early Church did at the Council of Carthage to this issue. We now continue on with the discussion, shifting specifically to biblical prophecy.

As a result of the above discussions on revelation, inspiration, infallibility, and inerrancy, this book is written based on a plenary view of Scripture in general and of prophecy specifically, with a literal-historical-grammatical hermeneutic (or method of interpretation). This translates to the *literal view (versus allegorical view) of interpretation of biblical prophecy.* This also includes interpreting Scripture literally, historically, grammatically, contextually (both immediate and broad contexts), authorially (based on the author of each book), and exegetically (based on the original intended meaning for the original audience, in the original language),[9] while still allowing for the use of parables, metaphors, figures of speech, poetry, and symbols to bring meaning to the text.[10]

Biblical prophecy may then be divided into two categories: forthtelling, God's message for the present or near future situation; and foretelling, God's message for the future.[11] Additionally, foretelling may be further divided into the following two sub-categories: prophecy, concerned with this-world events; and apocalyptic, concerned with other-world events relating to cosmic, final solutions.[12] The two primary examples of biblical apocalyptic prophecy are the Books of Daniel and Revelation, as well as major portions of Ezekiel, Zechariah, and portions of Isaiah.[13] Additionally, there remains Jesus' Apocalyptic Discourse recorded by Matthew, Mark, and Luke and various eschatological teachings of Paul, contained in his Epistles in the New Testament.

The following five general characteristics must also be understood about biblical prophecy: 1) Old Testament prophets understood history in two main periods, *the present age and the age to come*; 2) Old Testament prophets had a telescopic (very narrow) view of the future; 3) Old Testament prophecy may have two fulfillments, one near the prophet's lifetime, and another in the far distant future; 4) New Testament teaching focuses prophecy on *both comings of the Lord Jesus Christ*; and 5) Some prophecies are conditional, not absolute, and are based on God's sovereignty and the relationship between God and His people.[14] Next, the specifics of biblical prophecy will be discussed.

There are several methods of prophetic revelation. First of all there are *types*: for example, of Jesus—"the seed of the woman" in Genesis 3:15; "the prophet like Moses" in Deuteronomy 18:18; "the fourth man in the fiery furnace" in Daniel 3; and the "Son of Man" in Daniel 7:13. Next, there are *symbols*: for example, of the Holy Spirit—"pillar of cloud by day/fire by night" in Exodus; the "wind/breath of life" in Genesis 1–2 and John 3; and "the dove" at Jesus' baptism (Matt 3:16; Mark 1:10; Luke 3:21–22). Then, there are Jesus' *parables*: for example, the Parable of the Wheat and Weeds in Matthew 13 (regarding the true Gospel and Satan's false gospel coexisting until the end of the age). And finally, there are *dreams and visions*: for example, Ezekiel's vision in Ezekiel 1; Nebuchadnezzar's dream in Daniel 2; and John's vision in Revelation.[15] Yet, there remain the following general principles for interpreting prophecy: 1) "Interpret literally"; 2) Interpret in accordance with the "harmony of prophecy" (the "full counsel" of the Word of God); 3) "Observe the perspective and time relationship of the prophecy"; 4) Interpret historically, culturally, socially, and grammatically; 5) Interpret with a view toward possible double fulfillment; and overall 6) "Interpret consistently."[16] In other words, when interpreting biblical prophecy, we should interpret it *literally* first and foremost; and then, ensure that it is interpreted *contextually within the specific prophecy* as well as consistently in accordance with other biblical prophecy in the Scriptures.

For many cases in biblical prophecy, the interpretation is contained as a follow-on part of the text (e.g., Gen 41:1–36—Joseph interpreting Pharaoh's dream). However, if that is not the case, then two aids will be very helpful in determining the literal meaning. The first is using multiple translations of the Bible to interpret a specific passage of Scripture. This should be done by comparing multiple versions of the Bible along the spectrum of a very "literal" word-for-word translation to a more "dynamic" thought-for thought translation (e.g., New King James Version [NKJV], New American Standard Bible [NASB], New Revised Standard Version [NRSV], New International Version [NIV], Good News Bible [GNB], and New Living Translation [NLT])[17] to help interpret the text. Then, there is looking up the "key words" in the text in the original language (Hebrew for the Old Testament and Greek for the New Testament) in a concordance (each concordance is tied to a specific translation of the Bible; e.g., *Strong's Concordance* for the KJV/NKJV), Bible dictionary/ encyclopedia, or ultimately a lexicon (in the original language), to get the correct contextual translation of the words.[18] If a literal interpretation makes no literal sense, then proceed to use a reference/study Bible or concordance to find similar wording in the rest of the Bible, to maintain a consistent interpretation (e.g., Jer 51:7 and Zech 5 address the "spirit of Babylon/ Babylon the Harlot" of Rev 17–18; and Ezekiel's vision of "Cherubim" in Ezek 1:4–28; 10:1–22 correspond to the four Living Creatures of Rev 4).

With the Book of Revelation being the only entire book focused on apocalyptic prophecy surrounding the Second Coming of the Lord Jesus Christ, theologians have developed four main ways to interpret it: Preterist, Idealist, Historical, and Futurist.

The first three, in one way or another, range from an entirely allegorical interpretive method to a mixture of allegorical and literal interpretive methods. On the other hand, only the Futurist interpretation strives for a completely literal methodology of interpretation.[19] A brief discussion of each follows.

The Preterist view of Revelation is based on the Hebrew word *preterit*—past-perfect tense of the Latin *praeteritus*, meaning "gone by/past."[20] Therefore, people who hold this view believe that John wrote this book to the historical seven churches in Asia Minor (modern, Turkey), to encourage and comfort them during the dire persecution at the hands of the Roman Empire. The primary period of the severest persecution took place during Nero's reign (AD 54–68). Nero is generally considered by this view to be the first beast of Revelation 13, with "emperor worship" being the second beast of Revelation 13. Thus according to this view, all, or nearly all (excluding the Second Coming of Jesus) of the events that occur in the Book of Revelation occurred in the first century AD, just after the book was written by John on the Isle of Patmos (i.e., just prior to the destruction of Jerusalem and the Temple in AD 70).[21]

Preterism may be divided into two camps. The Full Preterist (also known as consistent, orthodox, or hyperpreterist) believes that Jesus returned in AD 70 in the clouds over Jerusalem to judge Israel for their unbelief, thus, fulfilling all the biblical prophecy in Revelation in AD 70. However, the Partial Preterist believes that although Jesus did return in the clouds over Jerusalem in AD 70, there will be a "future second coming, resurrection, and final judgment."[22] The original proponent for the Preterist view was Jesuit Luis de Alcazar (1554–1613). However, Daniel Whitby (1638–1726) made it a more popular view in conjunction with his postmillennial view of Christ's return[23] (after a period of peace on earth brought about by the Gospel converting the nations—more specifics will be given on

Postmillennialism in a later chapter). Today, the Preterist view remains a minority view of interpreting the Book of Revelation.

The Idealist view (also known as the "spiritualist" view, because it interprets the Book of Revelation spiritually or "symbolically") basically believes that the entire Book of Revelation was written to be a spiritual allegory of the battle of good versus evil or the Kingdom of God versus the kingdom of Satan.[24] This view started with "allegorical method" of interpreting Scripture from the Alexandrian School of Theology, espoused by Clement of Alexandria (AD 150–215) and Origen (AD 152–254), and furthered by Augustine (AD 354–430) and Jerome (AD 347–420).[25] However, this allegorical view of interpretation departed from the long-standing literal interpretation of the Old Testament Scriptures (e.g., by Ezra the Priest, Neh 8:1–8), continued by the Rabbis, Jesus and His Apostles (who wrote the New Testament Scriptures), and nearly all of the Early Church Fathers of the first three centuries of the Church.[26] The Idealist view also remains a minority view of interpreting the Book of Revelation today.

The Historical view is based on the belief that the Book of Revelation is written to be the entirety of Church History—beginning with the Seven Churches of Asia Minor of Revelation 2–3, and concluding with the Second Coming of the Lord Jesus Christ in Revelation 19–20. Therefore, adherents to this view look at events that have occurred throughout approximately the last two thousand years to specifically fulfill the events described by John in Revelation. The first proponent of this view was Joachim de Fiora[27] (1135–1202), a Roman Catholic Italian monk who divided history into three ages or dispensations: 1) The Father (or Law), from Creation to the Incarnation of Jesus; 2) The Son (or Grace), from Jesus' First Coming to His Second Coming (determined by de Fiora to be in the year 1260); and 3) The Holy Spirit (or Spiritual Church), for the Millennium (the one thousand-year reign of Christ on Earth of Rev 20) and into Eternity.[28] This view became very popular during the Reformation Period, because it claimed that the pope and the papacy were the two beasts of Revelation 13. Since that time, there have been "as many as fifty" proponents of this view who have given their personal interpretations of the historical fulfillments of the many, varied events outlined by the Book of Revelation.[29] Although the Historical view has a greater following than either the Preterist or Idealist today, it is still not the predominant view (probably due to its straying from the literal interpretive method of Scripture).

The final view of interpreting the Book of Revelation is the Futurist view, which holds to the literal method of interpreting Scripture and has the greatest following of adherents today. This view is also directly related to the premillennial view of Jesus' return (Jesus' Second Coming in Rev 19 precedes His one thousand-year reign in Rev 20—more will also be addressed on this in chapter 6). Thus, this literal interpretation is based on a literal rendering of Jesus' words to John in Revelation 1:19: "Write therefore the things which you have seen, and the things which are, and the things which shall take place after these things." It seems fairly clear that Jesus is commanding John to write (and thus, we are to read and interpret) the Book of Revelation in three separate segments: 1) things John saw, in Revelation 1–2; 2) things which are, in Revelation 2–3; and 3) things which are to come, in Revelation 4–22. Understood from this perspective then, Revelation 2–3 is not only speaking about the literal Seven Churches of Asia Minor of John's day, but about the entire "Church Age"—which we are still in today, and will remain in until the Rapture of the Church occurs per 1 Thessalonians 4:13–18 (more will also be addressed on this subject in chapter 8). Thus, the bulk of the Book of Revelation is referring to events that are to take place at some time in the future, just prior to the Second Coming of Jesus (which will specifically take place during the seven-year period, most commonly known as the Tribulation, per Dan 9:24–27; 12^{30}—again, more will be addressed on this in chapter 7). And since the two beasts of Revelation 13 have been mentioned as a point of reference in the other views, the Futurist view of these beasts will be addressed here for consistency's sake. Futurists believe these two beasts to be the political and religious heads of the future Tribulation world power or empire.[31] Other names have been given to these beasts: such as Antichrist and False Prophet. However, this subject will also be addressed in chapter 7.

From the discussion above regarding the literal over the allegorical method of interpreting Scripture in general and biblical prophecy specifically, it should be clear that the Futurist view is the preferred view to interpret the Book of Revelation. This provides not only a consistency within the book itself, but also a consistency with the many direct and indirect references to other portions of Scripture in both the Old and New Testaments. This also provides for the continuity of the whole counsel of the Word of God from beginning to end; alpha to omega; and Genesis to Revelation. With this discussion of biblical prophecy and its interpretation being finished, we now turn our attention to time and biblical timelines, to be addressed in the next chapter.

3.

Time and Timelines in the Bible

Understanding *Kairos* and *Chronos* Time, and Biblical & Salvation History

The concept of time was created for humanity by God in Genesis 1:14–19. However, God is love (1 John 4:8, 16), spirit (John 4:24), and light (1 John 1:5). And according to Albert Einstein's Theory of Relativity (and Time Dilation), as one travels faster and approaches the speed of light (approximately 186,000 miles per second), time slows down.[1] Then technically *at* the speed of light, *there is no time, just eternity or infinity.* Since God *is* light, and based on this understanding, it may be supposed that God *exists at the speed of light in eternity.* This seems to coincide with Moses' statement about God in Psalm 90:2, "Before the mountains were created, before you made the earth and the world, you are God, *without beginning or end* [emphasis added]" (NLT). As a result of this understanding, the purpose of time rests within God's creation (Prov 16:4; Eccl 8:6). It may be further developed from the Bible that time:

1) had a beginning (Gen 1:14);

2) is linear—proceeding since its creation in a line, not a circle—(Matt 28:18–20; Luke 3:23–38; 17:22–30; 21:7–28; Acts 1:1–11);

3) is finite, quantifiable, and measurable (Gen 1:14; 8:22; Gal 4:10);

4) is part of the space-time continuum (Dan 2:20–22, 28–45; 9:1–2, 24–27; 12:8–13; 2 Cor 12:1–4; Rev 1:9–19; 4:1–2); and

5) will end when its purpose is completed (Gen 8:22; Rev 21:1–6a).

The Old Testament biblical concept of time is communicated in Hebrew primarily by the word *et*, which can mean linear time, but more often is associated with specific events and is translated *kairos* in Greek.[2] The word *yom* is also used in Hebrew to communicate a unit of time, most often "day or today."[3] In Greek, the New Testament biblical concept of linear or chronological time is communicated primarily by the word *chronos* (from which is derived the word chronology, the study of time or history). This concept of time is understood "*quantitatively* [emphasis added] and measured by successive objects, events, or moments."[4] However, when God steps into time (or eternity coincides with time), it becomes *kairos* time, meaning, "season, opportune time, or time of accomplishment." This concept of time is understood "*qualitatively* [emphasis added] and is affected by influence or period of accomplishment." The plural form of *kairos* is translated "seasons," and means times at which certain foreordained (biblical prophetic) events take place. Specific examples of this plural form used in Scripture are "times of the Gentiles" in Luke 21:24, and "times and epochs" in 1 Thessalonians 5:1.[5]

The primary example of *kairos* time in Scripture is the Incarnation (God becoming flesh at the birth of Jesus Christ), spoken of as being "in the fullness of time" by Paul in Galatians 4:4 (which may be further understood as, "eternity stepping into time"). Some examples of *kairos* time from the Old Testament include:

1) God walking with Adam and Eve in the Garden of Eden before the Fall (Gen 1:27–3:24);

2) Enoch's rapture to heaven (Gen 5:21–24);

3) Noah's covenant with God (Gen 8:20–9:17);

4) Job's conversations with God (Job 38–42:9);

5) Abraham's covenant with God (Gen 12, 15, 17); his interaction with the three heavenly visitors (Gen 18); and God's provision and substitution of the ram for Isaac on Mt. Moriah (Gen 22:1–18);

6) Jacob wrestling with "the Angel" and being renamed Israel (Gen 32:24–32);

7) Moses talking with God—at the burning bush (Exod 3–4:16), during the Exodus (Exod 5–15), atop Mt. Sinai (Exod 19–31), and in the pillar of cloud and fire (Exod 40:34–38);

8) Joshua talking with the "Captain of the LORD's Army" (Josh 5:13–15); and

9) Elijah's rapture to heaven (2 Kgs 2:1–13).

Other examples of *kairos* time from the New Testament include the following:

1) Jesus Christ's baptism (Matt 3:13–17), transfiguration (Matt 17:1–13), crucifixion (Matt 27:32–55), resurrection (Matt 28:1–15), and ascension (Acts 1:1–11);

2) the coming of the Holy Spirit at Pentecost (Acts 2);

3) John's vision in the Book of Revelation; and in the future, and

4) Jesus' Second Coming and His Millennial Reign on earth (Rev 19–20:6).

Thus, it appears that the Garden of Eden, Jesus' life on earth, and the Millennium all show God's intent for *kairos* time and *chronos* time to coexist throughout all human existence.

There are other theological definitions of time based on its Old Testament understanding. One such main understanding is of God dealing with the chosen people through *covenants* (which will be addressed more specifically in the next chapter); dealing with the world through signs, wonders, and nature; and finally, dealing with humanity individually.[6] There are also other theological definitions of time based on its New Testament understanding. For example, there is a view related to people living in the present that is being shaped by the future of the coexistence of temporal (*chronos*) time and eternity (*kairos*), called a "Christian Shape to Time."[7] Then, there are views that separate created time (*chronos*) from the Creator's divine eternity (*kairos*). All these views encourage people to allow God to fit the *eschaton* (the end of time/history and the beginning of a new heaven/new earth) into His divine time for humanity.[8] Another view puts it this way: "to heed the psalmist's words, 'My times are in thy hand'" (Ps 31:15). This view allows humanity's time to have its basis in the "time of God."[9] The New Testament views of time deal with the intersection of *kairos* time with *chronos* time, <u>but primarily only at the point of the *eschaton*</u>, and not as coexisting with eternity in a cohesive, consistent, and continuing manner. Therefore, the understanding of *kairos* and *chronos* time, coexisting in a historical-prophetic, linear, and eschatological manner (with a future end in sight) is how the concept of time will be addressed hereafter. The specifics of biblical time will now be addressed.

Biblical time is centered on the purposes of God in relation to humanity, and is communicated through the concepts of Salvation History and the Kingdom of Heaven/God[10] (which will also be addressed in detail in the next chapter). The concept of "salvation" existed in the mind of the Triune God of the Bible (represented by the plural Hebrew name for God in Genesis, *Elohim*) before the foundation of the world (Eph 1:4), or the creation of Adam and Eve (who were made in the very image of God—without sin and considered to be "very good" vs. "good" for the rest of creation—Gen 1:26–31). However, Salvation History is set into context and begins immediately after the Original Sin of Adam and Eve (the Fall) in Genesis 3:15. Here, the promise of the virgin birth of the Messiah, literally translated "her seed" and "He/him" in the *Septuagint* (*the Greek translation of the Hebrew Bible*),[11] is found within the curse to the serpent: "And I will put enmity between you and the woman, and between your seed and *her seed*; *He* shall bruise you on the head, and you shall bruise *him* on the heel" [emphasis added].[12] Thus, the Christian orthodox doctrines of the Trinity and the seed and promise of the Messiah (Christ in Greek) for salvation (atonement) are outlined from the beginning of biblical time in Genesis.

In the Old Testament, biblical time is viewed as prophetic and looks forward to the Kingdom of Heaven/God coming through the Messiah (kingdom coming). In the New Testament, biblical time is viewed as apocalyptic—kingdom initiated by Jesus, but not fully realized until His *Parousia*/Second Coming at the *eschaton*. Apocalyptic time is previewed by Jesus' Apocalyptic Discourse on the Mount of Olives (Matt 24; Mark 13; Luke 21). However, apocalyptic time did not actually begin until after the completion of the Atonement by the resurrection of Jesus (which was the prophetic fulfillment of the Old Testament Messiah and beginning of the kingdom by Jesus). Apocalyptic time also looks forward to the Second Coming/*Parousia* of Jesus and the complete fulfillment of the Kingdom of Heaven/God on earth by His millennial reign as outlined by Revelation 11:15 and 19:11–20:4.[13] Therefore, it follows that when interpreting eschatological portions of Scripture, one must determine whether the context is prophetic eschatology or apocalyptic eschatology. The Old Testament and the Gospels are set in prophetic eschatological time—primarily pointing and relating to Jesus' First Coming. However, the rest of the New Testament is set in apocalyptic eschatological time—pointing to Jesus' Second Coming/*Parousia*.[14]

Jesus Christ—being the embodiment of Salvation History—after being introduced initially as "the seed of the woman" in Genesis, is then foreshadowed throughout the entire

Old Testament by themes or types in each book. There is, for example, "the Passover Lamb" in Exodus, "the High Priest" in Leviticus, "the pillar of cloud by day and pillar of fire by night" in Numbers, "the Prophet like Moses" in Deuteronomy, and "the Captain of the LORD's Host" in Joshua. Salvation History is then interwoven throughout the entire New Testament, and again, represented by different names for Jesus Christ in each book, for example: "Messiah" in Matthew, "Wonderworker" in Mark, "the Son of Man" in Luke, and "the Son of God" in John.[15]

Salvation History is also addressed by God with specific salvation acts on behalf of the Children of Israel in the Old Testament as follows:

> 1) The Exodus out of Egypt and through the Red Sea (Exod 12:31–15:21);
>
> 2) The protection, provision, and leading for forty years in the wilderness (Num 13–33);
>
> 3) The conquering and resettling in the promised land of Canaan (the Book of Joshua);
>
> 4) The deliverance from surrounding nations during the time of the Judges and Kings (the Books of Judges; 1 and 2 Sam; 1 and 2 Kgs); and
>
> 5) The Post-Exilic return and rebuilding of the nation of Israel (the Books of Ezra and Neh).

Salvation History is then specifically addressed in the messianic prophecies of the Old Testament prophets (e.g., Isa 7:14; 9:6–7; 52:13–53; 61:1–11; Dan 7:13–14; 9:20–27; Mic 5:2–15; Mal 3:1–6; 4:1–4). Most of these prophecies were confirmed and sealed by the New Testament writers as being fulfilled by Jesus during His First Coming (e.g., Matt 1:21–23; Luke 18:32; Acts 8:32–35; Luke 3:21–22; 4:16–21; Matt 9:6; 12:8, 32, 40; 16:13; Matt 2:6; John 7:42; Luke 24:25–27; Acts 2:22–36).[16] This was done while looking toward the consummation of history and salvation at the *Parousia*/Second Coming of Jesus (e.g., Matt 24; Mark 13; Luke 17 and 21; Rom 8:1–30; 1 Cor 15; Phil 1:6; 1 Thess 4:13–5:24; Rev 19:10–21).[17] The Second Coming/*Parousia* of Jesus is the subject of chapter 5, and will be further addressed in detail there.

Thus for our purposes here, the concept of *chronos* time will be considered to be historical-chronological-prophetic time, which began with the creation of the sun, moon, and stars on day four in Genesis 1:14–19 and will end with the creation of a "new heaven and new earth" in Revelation 21–22. So, the year 2019 corresponds to the year 5779 per the Jewish calendar; to the year 6023 per the best combined estimate from the Julian, Gregorian, and Bishop Ussher's calendars;[18] and to the year 6019–6020 per Michael Rood's newly discovered Astronomically and Agriculturally Corrected Biblical Hebrew Calendar.[19] And, biblical time (both prophetic and apocalyptic eschatological) and Salvation History will be viewed as *kairos* time brought into focus with how it intersects with and in *chronos* time. With that foundation laid, we shall now address what the Bible has to say about specific prophetic timelines.

The overarching prophetic timeline, addressing all the concepts of time above, is believed to be patterned after the "Creation Week" in Genesis 1:1–2:3 (including the seventh day of rest established by God, later known to the Israelites as the Sabbath [*Shabbat*]).[20] Factoring in the concept that "a day with the Lord" is literally "one thousand years" (Ps 90:4; 2 Pet 3:8), many of the Early Church Fathers believed that humanity's lease on earth was six thousand years. This was to be followed by God's sabbath rest of one thousand years, or the Millennium of Revelation 20.[21] Thus, the entire overarching prophetic Creation Week Timeline is seven thousand years. *A note must be made at this point.* Although there are many different views of creation and associated timelines, the merits of each would provide too lengthy a discussion, with little definitive resolution to be made, and thus, will not be addressed here. However, the following is provided as a "Five-Tiered Model"[22] on the subject, covering the spectrum of "creation to evolution":

1) Young Earth Creationism (also known as Biblical Creationism/Scientific Creationism),[23]

2) Old Earth Creationism (related to the Day-Age Theory, Intelligent Design, and also known as Old Earth Episodic Creationism/Progressive Creationism),[24]

3) Evolutionary Creationism (also known as Theistic Evolution),[25]

4) Evolutionary Deism (related to Process Theology and also known as Deistic Evolution),[26] and

5) Evolutionary Materialism (also known as Evolutionary Naturalism, Scientism, or Scientific Secularism).[27]

Suffice it to say that from a prophetic timeline point of view, the overarching prophetic Creation Week Timeline mentioned above is the most agreed upon in Church History and my thirty-five years of research on the subject. Therefore, we will use it as the basis for this prophetic timeline discussion. Next, there are several prophetic sub-timelines that break down prophetic time for both the Jews and Gentiles.

The seven annual Jewish Biblical Feasts or Festivals of Leviticus 23 and Numbers 28–29 (Passover, Unleavened Bread, Firstfruits, Weeks or Pentecost, Trumpets, Day of Atonement, and Tabernacles or Booths) prophetically focus on a timeline of both comings of the Messiah for the Jews.[28] The first four of these feasts were prophetically fulfilled during the First Coming of Messiah—by Jesus' death, burial, resurrection, and His sending of the Holy Spirit to empower the Church (His Body). The Feast of Passover is fulfilled by Jesus' death as the sacrificial lamb (Lev 23:5—Matt 26:2; John 19:14; 1 Cor 5:7).

The Feast of Unleavened Bread is fulfilled by Jesus' body buried in the tomb/earth for three days and three nights per Matthew 12:39–40 (Lev 23:6–7—Mark 14:22; John 6:51; 1 Cor 10:16). The Feast of Firstfruits is fulfilled by Jesus' resurrection (Lev 23:10–11—Mark 16:1–6; John 20:1, 19–23; 1 Cor 15:20–23). And, the Feast of Weeks (Pentecost) is fulfilled by Jesus sending the promised Holy Spirit to empower the newly created Church/Body of Christ (Lev 23:15–16—Acts 1:1–5, 8; 2:1–4). Then, there is a **"gap"** of approximately four months (per Jesus' prophetic words in John 4:34–38) in the annual calendar between these four feasts in the spring and the last three feasts in the fall. This **gap** may be prophetically construed as **the Church Age or the Times of the Gentiles** (Luke 21:24; Rom 11:25) between the two comings of Messiah Jesus.[29]

So, what remains of these seven Old Testament annual feasts is the apocalyptic eschatological fulfillment of the last three feasts (Trumpets, Atonement, and Booths or Tabernacles) at the time of the *Parousia* of Jesus. The Feast of Trumpets will be fulfilled by Jesus returning in the clouds for His Body (the Rapture of the Church), at the beginning of the *Parousia* (Lev 23:23–25—1 Thess 4:14–17; Luke 21:36; Acts 1:8–11). The Feast of Atonement will then be fulfilled when Jesus judges the earth/humanity for their sins during the Day of the LORD/*Yahweh* (Tribulation/Armageddon) at the end of the *Parousia* (Lev 23:26–27—Matt 24:9–22; Rev 5–19). Finally, the Feast of Booths will be fulfilled by the Messianic Kingdom on earth during the Millennium (Lev 23:34, 42–43—Ezek 43:1–12; Joel 3:18–21; Mic 4:1–8; Zeph 3:11–20; Zech 14:4–16; Rev 20:2–4).[30] Please note that all three of these apocalyptic eschatological concepts will be addressed in detail by subsequent chapters in this book. After these last three Old Testament feasts are fulfilled through the *Parousia* and the Millennium, all seven annual Biblical Feasts of Israel will have been fulfilled by or through *Yeshua HaMashiach* (Jesus the Messiah/Christ).

There is also a Jewish sub-timeline and a Gentile sub-timeline contained in the Book of Daniel. In Daniel 9, God reveals to Daniel the timeline for His people, the Jews, intertwined with both the First and Second Comings of the Messiah and the coming of the Messianic Kingdom. This is conveyed in the "Seventy-sevened," or Seventy Weeks, of Years (70 x 7 = 490 years) Prophecy. The Angel Gabriel explains to Daniel in verse 24 that the prophecy is for "your people (Jews) and your holy city (Jerusalem):

> 1) to finish the transgression (70-year exile prophecy of Jer 25:11–12; 29:10),
>
> 2) to make an end of sin (Messiah's First and Second Comings),
>
> 3) to make atonement for iniquity (Messiah's First Coming),
>
> 4) to bring in everlasting righteousness (Messiah's Second Coming),
>
> 5) to seal up vision and prophecy (Messiah's Second Coming), and
>
> 6) to anoint the most holy place (Messiah's First and Second Comings)."

In Daniel 9:25, Daniel is told that "from a decree to restore and rebuild Jerusalem" (which is traditionally understood to have been issued by Artaxerxes Longimanus, and addressed by Nehemiah 2:5–8, in 445–444 BC)[31] "until Messiah the Prince" (First Coming) there will be "seven weeks and sixty-two weeks" (69 weeks of years = 483 years) …. Then (after the 69 weeks), "the *Messiah will be cut off and have nothing, or but not for himself* [emphasis added] (The Interlinear Bible).[32] This is speaking of the crucifixion and atonement of the Messiah during His First Coming. However, the question remains: Was this prophecy fulfilled literally and exactly? Taking 444–445 BC as the starting point and adding 483 years, leaves a chronological date of approximately AD 38–39. Factoring in the Gregorian Calendar being off by four to six years (due to the miscalculation of the year of the birth of Jesus Christ and that in this system there must be both a 1 BC and an AD 1)[33] leaves a revised chronological date of anywhere from AD 31–35. Since Jesus' age at His death was 33, this falls within this range of dates, and, thereby, exactly fulfills this part of the prophecy! *As an additional note*: According to Luke 3:1, the start of Jesus' ministry was in the year AD 28—fifteenth year of Tiberius Caesar.[34] Then by adding the traditionally accepted three-plus year ministry of Jesus, we arrive at the year AD 31 for His death (although, according to Frederick A. Larson and The Star of Bethlehem Documentary 2007, Jesus died in the year AD 33).[35]

Daniel 9:26 then continues, "…and the people of the prince who is to come will destroy the city and the sanctuary." This specific prophecy was fulfilled by the Romans in AD 70.[36] Then, there is the **gap** in the timeline, representative of the **Times of the Gentiles/Church Age**. And finally in verse 27, there remains a "*he*," who "will make a firm covenant with the many for one week" (remaining 7 years of the 490 prophesied, or *Daniel's Seventieth Week*). And "in the middle of the week (3½ years), he will put a stop to sacrifice and grain offering." This is speaking of the future Antichrist and the seven-year Tribulation Period (broken into two 3½-year periods, with the latter period called the "Great Tribulation"), which are outlined in Revelation 4–18, and precede the Second Coming of Messiah Jesus (Rev 19:11–21).[37] This particular Jewish timeline prophecy regarding the future Antichrist is further refined by Daniel 11:40–45. This section of Scripture begins with the phrase, "And at the *end time* [emphasis added] . . ." and ends with, "…yet he will come to his end, and no one will help him." Again, all these concepts will be developed further in subsequent chapters.

Continuing the prophecy from the end of Daniel 11, Daniel 12:1a states: "Now at that time Michael, the great prince who stands guard over the sons of your people, will arise. And there will be a time of distress such as never occurred since there was a nation until that time . . ." (the Great Tribulation). This Great Tribulation will last for 3½ years: "from the time that the regular sacrifice is abolished and the abomination of desolation is set up, there will be 1,290 days" (Dan 12:11). This is the same 3½ years spoken of in Daniel 9:27: "in the middle of the week he will put a stop to sacrifice . . ." Daniel 12:1b also speaks of the *resurrection of the Old Testament Saints*: "and at that time your people, everyone who is found written in the book, will be rescued. And many of those who sleep in the dust of the ground will awake, these to everlasting life, but the others to disgrace and everlasting contempt." Then in the following verses, God provides closure to the Jewish sub-timeline, an answer to Daniel's question, "What will be the outcome of these events?" (Dan 12:8b), and encouragement that He is in control: "And from the time that the regular sacrifice is abolished, and the abomination of desolation is set up, there will be 1,290 days. *How blessed is he who keeps waiting and attains to the 1,335 days* [emphasis added]" (Dan 12:11–12). This is representative of Jesus' literal, visible, and physical Second Coming described in Revelation 19:11–21. Next, we will look at the Gentile sub-timeline in Daniel.

The Gentile sub-timeline, mentioned in Daniel 2 and 7, and more specifically broken down by Daniel 8, 10, and 11, is represented by Nebuchadnezzar's statue made of different materials and by the four beasts to arise out of the earth. Each metal (in decreasing order of value) and beast represents a kingdom that will rule over Israel. The "head of gold" and "lion with wings of an eagle" represent Nebuchadnezzar's Babylonian Empire (Dan 2:38; 7:4). The "breast and arms of silver," "bear raised up on one side with three ribs in its mouth," and "ram with two horns" represent the Medes and Persian Empire (Dan 2:39; 5:28; 7:5; 8:3–4, 20). The "belly and thighs of bronze," "leopard with four wings like a bird and four heads," and "shaggy goat with a conspicuous horn broken off and replaced with four horns" represent the Grecian Empire of Alexander the Great, later broken into four smaller kingdoms (Dan 2:39; 7:6; 8:5–8, 21–22; 10:20; 11:2–3). The "legs of iron" and "fourth beast which was terrifying, extremely strong, and had large iron teeth" represent the Roman Empire (Dan 2:40; 7:7, 23), in which Christianity was declared to be the religion of the Empire by Emperor Constantine (AD 313),[38] and eventually was divided into the East (Constantinople) and West (Rome) empires/churches in 1054.[39] And again, there remain the **Times of the Gentiles/Church Age Gap**.

This **gap** remains until the Rapture of the Church (1 Thess 4:13–18) at its terminus and the rise of the Antichrist. At that time, the fifth and final kingdom made up of "the feet and toes of iron mixed with clay" and "ten horns on the fourth beast"—representing a Ten-Nation Confederacy from the confines of the Old Roman Empire—will arise (Dan 2:44; 7:7b–8, 24). This Ten-Nation Confederacy is understood to be either a revived Roman Empire (i.e., the Common Market, EEC, or EEU),[40] or a Ten-Nation Arab Confederacy, based on those nations described as enemies of Israel and seeking to destroy it as a nation (outlined by Ps 83). These ten Old Testament nations (Edom, the Ishmaelites, Moab, the Hagrites or Hagarenes, Gebal, Ammon, Amalek, Philistia/the Philistines, Tyre, and Assyria/Assur) make up parts of, or all of, the following modern Arab countries that surround Israel: Jordan, Saudi Arabia, Kuwait, Iraq, Egypt, Lebanon, the Palestinians (PLO), Syria, Iran, and Turkey.[41] Most parts of these modern nations fall within the confines of the Old Roman Empire.[42] And, all but Iran and Turkey are part of the Arab League (founded in 1945, and whose explicit, first and foremost, goal is the destruction of Israel).[43] In light of this information and the world events occurring in the Middle East since the close of WWII, it appears that the Ten-Nation Arab Confederacy (from Ps 83) is the more likely choice for fulfillment of Daniel's fifth kingdom. More is then provided concerning these Gentile kingdoms and the revealing of the Antichrist in subsequent visions of Daniel 8, 10, and 11.

In Daniel 8, this Gentile timeline has additional specific prophecies pertaining to the partitioning of the Grecian Empire after Alexander the Great's death (at the age of 32)[44] into "four horns" (Dan 8:8), representing four kingdoms (Dan 8:22). Then, "out of one of them came forth a rather small horn" (Dan 8:9)—representing "…in the latter period of their rule …a king will arise" (Dan 8:23), who will "desecrate the holy place (Second Temple)" (Dan 8:11–12), and "stop the regular sacrifice …for 2,300 evenings and mornings" (Dan 8:14). In Daniel 11:4, the "four horns" of Daniel 8 are further clarified to be, "parceled out toward the four points of the compass (north, east, south, and west), though not to his descendants." This is representative of Alexander's four generals to whom the Grecian Empire was divided. These four generals were Lysimachus, Cassander, Seleucus, and Ptolemy. Lysimachus received Thrace and most of Asia Minor (modern Turkey). Cassander received Macedonia and Greece. Ptolemy received Egypt, Palestine, Cilicia (southeastern province of Asia Minor), Petra (modern Jordan), and Cyprus. And, Seleucus received the rest of Asia: Syria, Babylon, Persia, and India.[45] The Northern Kingdom (the Seleucids of Syria) and the Southern Kingdom (the Ptolemies of Egypt) then engaged in many battles and wars in a struggle for power (Dan 11:5–20). This ends with a Syrian king fulfilling the prophecy in Daniel 8:9 about the "small horn." This is further clarified to be when his forces set "up the abomination of desolation" in the "sanctuary" (Dan 11:31). This specific prophecy was fulfilled by Antiochus IV (Epiphanes) during his reign, 175–164 BC (most probably 167–164 BC, counting both the evening and morning sacrifices occurring in one day, thus, dividing the 2,300 into 1,150 days).[46]

Next, the prophecy in Daniel 11:40–45 goes on to speak of "the end time," when *one like Antiochus Epiphanes* [emphasis added] will "enter the Beautiful Land, and many countries will fall …. But he will gain control over the hidden treasures of gold and silver…he will go forth with great wrath to destroy and annihilate many …. And he will pitch the tents of his royal pavilion between the seas and the beautiful Holy Mountain; yet he will come to his end and no one will help him." This is speaking of the Antichrist, who will arise at the time of the Ten-Nation Confederacy, during the Seven-Year Tribulation described by Daniel's Seventieth Week (Dan 9:27 and Rev 4–18). And finally, we return back to Daniel 2:44 for closure of the Gentile prophetic sub-timeline, relative to the Kingdom of Heaven/God: "And in the days of those kings (the ten kings of the Ten-Nation Confederacy) *the God of heaven will set up a kingdom which will never be destroyed, and that kingdom will not be left for another people; it will crush and put an end to all these kingdoms, but it will itself endure forever* [emphasis added]." This is a description of the Messianic or Millennial Kingdom of Jesus described in Revelation 20:1–6, immediately after Jesus' Second Coming described previously in Revelation 19:11–21.

Thus in the final analysis, Jesus Christ is truly the beginning, end (Alpha and Omega—Rev 21:6), and middle (or centrality, based on His death, resurrection, and ascension) of all time and the biblical timelines. In fact, it has been said in Christian circles *that Jesus Christ*, aside from being both the written Word of God (attested to from Genesis to Revelation in the Bible) and the living Word of God in the flesh (John 1:1–14), *is also the center focal point of all human history*, making it

"His"—"story." And as mentioned above, this discussion on time and biblical timelines logically flows into the topic for the next chapter—the Kingdom of Heaven/God and how it relates to Biblical Covenants.

4.

Kingdom of Heaven, Kingdom of God
How Does the Kingdom Pertain to Biblical Covenants?

As mentioned in the previous chapter, biblical time is centered on the purposes of God in relation to humanity, and is communicated through the concepts of Salvation History and the Kingdom of Heaven (God).[1] In Hebrew, the phrase "Kingdom of Heaven" is rendered *malkut shamayim*,[2] and in Greek, *basileia ton ouranon*.[3] Again in Greek, "Kingdom of God" is rendered, *basileia tou theou*. However, there is no corresponding phrase in Hebrew for Kingdom of God, because Jews do not allow themselves to speak, or even write, the name of God (*Yahweh, Elohim*, etc.) in Hebrew. Instead, they replace all biblical references to God with LORD (*Adonai*). This concept appears to be based on the "kingly rule of Yahweh—first of all through Torah in the hearts of men, and secondly, physically on the earth through His chosen people."[4] Also, the Kingdom of Heaven is viewed as the spiritual or supernatural realm where God is and rules sovereignly.[5] Thus, both terms—Kingdom of Heaven and Kingdom of God—are synonymous, biblically and theologically meaning the same thing.

The concept of the Kingdom of Heaven/God is not mentioned in those exact words in the Old Testament. However, the concepts of promise, election, deliverance, covenant, law, land, and ultimately, the establishment of the office structure of prophet, priest, and king for the Nation of Israel speak directly to this same idea. Specifically regarding the Kingdom of Heaven/God in the Old Testament, there exists "a contrast between the present order of things and the redeemed order of the Kingdom of God…this age and the Age to Come…probably representing the Hebrew *olam habbah*."[6] This dual distinction was derived from the Old Testament prophets' understanding of history. This was outlined in chapter 2, and is partially repeated here for convenience's sake. There are two main periods of time, "the present age" and "the age to come"; a telescopic (very narrow) view of the future; and prophecies may have two fulfillments, one near the prophet's lifetime, and another in the far distant future.[7] The Hebrew word *olam* can also be translated "world or universe." The ancient rabbis spoke of two *olamot* or worlds: this world and the next, the world to come. So in rabbinic tradition, *olam habbah* can speak of either the afterlife or life in messianic times.[8]

Also in relation to the Old Testament view of the Kingdom of Heaven/God, "There is a twofold emphasis on God's kingship. He is frequently spoken of as the King, both of Israel (Exod 15:18; Num 23:21; Deut 33:5; Isa 43:15) and of all the earth (2 Kgs 19:15; Isa 6:5; Jer 46:18; Pss 29:10; 99:1–4)," in a spiritual sense. And, although God "is *now viewed*" as King from a Hebraic perspective, "other references speak of a day when He *shall become* King and *shall rule* over His people [emphasis added] (Isa 24:23; 33:22; 52:7; Zeph 3:15; Zech 14:9ff)."[9] This leads to the conclusion that while God *is* the King *spiritually*, He will *also become* King *physically* (i.e., He will *manifest* His kingship in the world of humanity and nations).[10] While there is an eschatological/teleological element in these descriptions of the Old Testament view of the Kingdom of Heaven/God, this can definitely be confirmed through the Book of Daniel[11] and apocalyptic Judaism (written from ca. 535–400 BC–the 2nd century AD).[12]

While there are various Hebrew words used for kingdom (146

times in the Old Testament), most of these refer to earthly kingdoms, and only a few refer to God's kingdom (Chronicles, 1; Psalms, 5; Isaiah, 2; Daniel, 7).[13] Overall, the biblical concept of kingdom has at least five different understandings. *First*, there is *God's universal kingdom*—"His overall, invisible, and everlasting reign over the entire universe." *Second*, there is *Jesus Christ's messianic kingdom*—a "visible, earthly, political kingdom promised to Israel, in which Messiah reigns over the whole earth from a throne in Jerusalem"—*this corresponds to the Millennial Kingdom of Revelation 20* (specifically addressed in chapter 6). *Third*, there is *God's spiritual kingdom (in the broad sense), including both good and evil—announced by Jesus in Matthew 13*, "and sometimes called the mystery form of the kingdom." *Fourth*, there is *God's spiritual kingdom (in the narrow sense), God's invisible reign only in the hearts of believers*—"this began when the first person was saved (John 3:3, 5) and will continue throughout eternity." And *fifth* and final, there is *God's "spiritual reign in the Church*—Peter used 'the keys of the kingdom' (Matt 16:19) to open the door of the Church to the Jews (Acts 2; 11:15) and to the Gentiles (Acts 10)."[14] Of these five understandings of the Kingdom of Heaven/God, the first three apply here. And although the first and third are alluded to in the Old Testament, the *second—Jesus' Messianic/Millennial Kingdom—is the one specifically prophesied about and which will now be addressed.*

Jacob ("he deceives"), whose name was changed to Israel ("one who struggles with God") by God (Gen 32:27–28), prophesies about his descendants in Genesis 49:10, and speaks of the kingly rule coming through the tribe of Judah: "until Shiloh (the one who brings peace—Messiah) comes"; and then, "And to him shall be the obedience of the peoples" (speaking of the Messianic Kingdom). In Exodus 19:6, God describes the Israelites under the Mosaic Covenant as "a kingdom of priests and a holy nation," thereby creating a true theocracy with God as their king. In Deuteronomy 17:14–20, God tells Moses that when the Israelites enter the Promised Land of Canaan they will desire a human king to rule them, and He lays out the rules for choosing that king. However as a parenthetical note, and getting back to God's desire for a theocratic kingdom for His chosen people, in the very next chapter of Deuteronomy (Deut 18:15, 18–19), God prophetically speaks through Moses to the Israelites about a "prophet like me [Moses]," whom He will raise up in the future that "you must listen to" (prophetically speaking of the coming of the Messiah as part of the Kingdom of Heaven/God).

Returning to the concession of God for a human king to rule over Israel, God confirmed this to Samuel before choosing Saul as the first human King of Israel (1 Sam 8:5–22). Then in 2 Samuel 7:12–17, God establishes a covenant with David: "I will raise up your descendent after you, who will come forth from you, and I will establish his kingdom…and *I will establish the throne of his kingdom forever…. And your house and your kingdom shall endure before me forever; your throne shall be established forever* [emphasis added]." David descended from the tribe of Judah (Matt 1:1, 3–6), beginning the fulfillment of Jacob's (Israel) prophecy in Genesis 49. And, God here specifies that the Messianic Kingdom would also come from the lineage of David (Matt 1:6–17).

Next in the Old Testament prophets, Isaiah mentions the coming of the Messiah and His reign several times in 9:6, 11:11–12, 24:3, and 32:1. Jeremiah speaks of the Messianic Covenant God will make with the Israelites in 31:31–33. Amos 9:11 talks about repairing and restoring "David's fallen tent," and to "build it as it used to be," addressing the future messianic reign. Micah 4:7–8 speaks of the restored Messianic Kingdom as also being political: "The LORD will rule over them in Mount Zion from that day and forever…the former dominion will be restored to you; kingship will come to the Daughter of Jerusalem."[15] Additionally, the prophet Joel speaks as if "the 'valley of decision' represents the place of the grand finale of the war between the *kingdom of God and the kingdom of the world* [emphasis added]."[16] And finally in Daniel, the only Old Testament apocalyptic prophetic book, the eschatological/ teleological Kingdom of Heaven/God (compared to earthly kingdoms) appears to be the central theme.[17]

The final section of prophecies that addresses the Kingdom of Heaven/God in the Old Testament relates to the restoration of Israel as God's chosen people and the establishment of the Messianic Millennial Kingdom. Some of these prophecies are located in the same passages of Scripture noted above.[18] Next, there are those scriptures that separately speak only of the coming Millennial Kingdom: Psalms 45; 68; 89; Joel 3:17–21;[19] and Psalms 72:1–8; 79:13; 113:4–9; and 145.[20] Finally, there are those passages that deal only with the restoration of Israel, Jerusalem, and the Temple.[21]

From all of the above testimony, it may be concluded that the Kingdom of Heaven/God is an eschatological/teleological term not only addressed by the Old Testament, but prophesied to come to pass in conjunction with the coming of the Messiah. And from the frame of reference of the twenty-first century, this would include both the First Coming and the Second Coming (*Parousia*—see chapter 5) of Jesus Christ (*Yeshua HaMashiach*). Therefore, there exists a very strong connection between the prophesied eschatological/teleological Messianic Kingdom and the Perfect/Complete Gospel of Both Comings of Jesus Christ. This is confirmed by Jesus and His ministry and the continuation of that ministry by the Apostles in New Testament times. The following New Testament scriptures connect the Old Testament to the New Testament in this regard, and provide a source of continuity of the Perfect/Complete

Gospel with the words "before the foundation of the world": Matthew 25:34; John 17:24; Ephesians 1:4–6; Hebrews 4:3; 9:26; 1 Peter 1:18–21; and Revelation 13:8; 17:8.

Jesus spent much of His time on earth teaching about the Kingdom of Heaven/God, saying that the kingdom came through Him.[22] And, *the Kingdom of Heaven/God (viewed through a teleological lens) is the kingdom come through Jesus' First Coming, but not fully yet, until His Second Coming (Parousia).*[23] Jesus, as well as other first-century rabbis, would have been aware of the eschatological concepts of the coming of Messiah, the Kingdom of the Heavens, the Day of the LORD (*Yahweh*), and the restoration of Israel from Daniel, Ezekiel, the Postexilic Prophets, and the writer of Chronicles.[24] Jesus would have also been aware of the other non-biblical, intertestamental (400 "silent years" between the Old and New Testaments) eschatological writings of the time, such as: 1 Enoch, the *Sibylline Oracles* (Book 3), *Psalms of Solomon, Jubilees, The Assumption of Moses*, 2 Baruch, 4 Ezra (Edras), *Apocalypse of Abraham,* and many of the Qumran Dead Sea Scrolls.[25] Both the Qumran Community and John the Baptist (who many believe was connected with the Qumran Community and who was Jesus' cousin) were contemporaries of Jesus, who also held a strongly apocalyptic eschatological view of the kingdom.[26]

When surveying the Gospels for Jesus' teachings, most theologians conclude that the primary thrust of Jesus' message was the Kingdom of Heaven/God per Matthew 4:12–17, 23; 9:35; Mark 1:14–15; and Luke 4:43; 8:1; 9:11.[27] Most of these teachings on the kingdom are contained in the Kingdom Parables (Matt 13:3–50; 18:23–35; 20:1–16; 22:1–14; 25:1–13; Mark 4:26–34; Luke 13:18–21; 19:11–27) or the Sayings of Jesus (Matt 5:3–20; 6:25–33; 7:13–29; 8:11–12; 11:11–19; 12:23–37; 18:1–14; 19:13–30; Luke 17:20–37; John 3:3–21). *This body of teaching also addresses the kingdom as having already come, in and through Jesus Christ spiritually, but would not be fully realized physically until the End of the Age.*[28]

Speaking of the parables of Jesus, "Probably one-third of all the recorded words of Jesus in the Synoptic Gospels are uttered in parables," and they should best be understood in their Second Temple Jewish context[29] (515 BC–AD 70), or *Sitz im Leben* (German for "original setting in life").[30] Although the kingdom could be understood in Jewish terms as being eschatological/ teleological, the direct application was living a holy, obedient life in the here and now to enter the kingdom after death.[31] With this explanation as a backdrop, Jesus' teachings on the Kingdom of Heaven/God will now be specifically considered.

The "mystery" of the kingdom was communicated by Jesus in the following parables: the Sower (Four Soils); the Wheat and the Tares (Weeds); the Mustard Seed; the Yeast (Leaven); the Hidden Treasure; the Pearl; the Net (all of these are contained in Matthew 13); and the Seed (Mark 4:26–29). Of these parables, the Wheat and Weeds and the Net both have eschatological/ teleological implications about judgment at "the End of the Age," while the others speak of the present spiritual kingdom during the Church Age.[32] Actually, the Parable of the Wheat and Weeds speaks to both this present Church Age Kingdom (vs. Satan's kingdom of darkness) and the judgment at the End of the Age. Additionally, the Parable of the Talents (Pounds) in Luke 19:11–27 speaks of stewardship in the Church Age,[33] between both comings of the Lord Jesus Christ.[34]

There are four more parables that speak of the Perfect/Complete Gospel of the Kingdom, the last two of which are definitely eschatological in nature. These four parables are addressed as follows: 1) the Unforgiving Servant (Matt 18:23–35), speaking of forgiveness;[35] 2) the Fair Employer (Matt 20:1–16), speaking of God's goodness, grace, and equality in the kingdom;[36] 3) the Great Banquet (Matt 22:2–14; Luke 14:15–24), speaking of the urgent invitation or call to all to enter the kingdom (especially the Jews); however, "many are called, but few are chosen" because of their response;[37] and 4) the Ten Maidens (Virgins) in Matt 25:1–13, speaking of the *Parousia*/Coming of Jesus for judgment at the End of the Age.[38]

There are those who believe (of whom I am one) that the Parable of the Ten Maidens (Virgins) and the Parable of the Talents (which follows in Matthew 25:14–30) are specifically speaking about the *judgment of Israel alone*.[39] Following these two parables in Matthew 25, and on the same eschatological note, is the Parable of the Sheep and the Goats (vv. 31–46). There has been much debate as to whether it should be considered a parable, a parabolic reference in Jesus' explanation of judgment connected with His *Parousia*, or just an apocalyptic eschatological statement.[40] In any case, it is contained in the eschatological Olivet Discourse of Jesus (Matt 24–25), follows two previous parables (at least one of which definitely speaks of eschatological judgment), and finishes the discourse with the theme of an eternal judgment. Much has been written about the interpretation of these verses, but all agree that they have to do with judgment in one form or another. My conclusion, after researching and writing on the subject,[41] is that *the Parable of the Sheep and the Goats represents the judgment of the Gentile nations that remain after the Tribulation, Battle of Armageddon, and the judgment of Israel preceding it.*[42]

Related to these verses, and again speaking of the eschatological/teleological nature of the kingdom, are Jesus' words found in Matthew 16:27–28: "For the Son of Man is going to come in the glory of His Father with His angels; and will then recompense every man according to his deeds. Truly I say to you, there are some of those who are standing here who shall not taste death until they see the Son of Man coming in His kingdom." This preview of the *Parousia*, described here, was seen by Peter, James, and John immediately following this (Matt 17) on the Mount of Transfiguration (and later by John in the vision on Patmos, recorded in Rev 19). Next, the Sayings of Jesus will be addressed, relating to the Kingdom of Heaven/ God.

The Sayings of Jesus regarding the kingdom may be divided into three categories: proclamation, teaching, and controversy.[43] Of the list of ten sayings mentioned above, only three speak of the spiritual kingdom of the Church Age being "here and now" exclusively (Matt 5:3–20; 6:25–33; 11:11–19). John 3:3–21 speaks of the spiritual kingdom, but in eschatological terms. The remainder speak of the kingdom being *both* now (in the Church Age) and in the future (in the Age to Come/*olam habbah*).[44]

The account of Jesus giving the Apostles and seventy or seventy-two disciples power (*dunamis* in Greek) and authority (*exousia* in Greek) over all of Satan's kingdom, and then commissioning them to go "proclaim the kingdom of God" (as a practical training exercise under His tutelage) is contained in Matthew 10, Luke 9:1–6, 10; and 10:1–24.[45] In the explanation, Jesus teaches them about the Kingdom of Heaven/God. Again, Jesus refers to both the present ("is at hand") and future ("until the Son of Man comes") teleological nature of the kingdom.[46]

Therefore, in addition to the conclusion above regarding the Old Testament view of Kingdom of Heaven/God, the testimony of the words of Jesus leads one to believe that He taught about an eschatological/teleological kingdom that was present then, now, until the end of the Church Age through the power of the Holy Spirit, and will be consummated by the Millennial Messianic Kingdom. Thus, the Kingdom of Heaven/God in this Present Age (period between both comings of Jesus) belongs to the Church (Matt 13 and Rev 2–3). As addressed previously, Matthew 13 (in the Parables of the Sower (Seed) and the Wheat and Weeds) illustrates the nature of the kingdom (compared to Satan's kingdom) during the Church Age.

In Revelation 2–3, Seven Periods of the Church Age appear to be prophetically addressed, in addition to the actual words for the existing seven churches in Asia Minor (modern Turkey) at the time the Apostle John penned the words of Revelation (ca. AD 96). Although this concept is controversial, many theologians have written on the subject and compiled the following "prophetic outline" of the Seven Periods of the Church Age:

> 1) Ephesus—the Birth of the Church (ca. AD 31) to the destruction of Jerusalem/the Temple and the continuity of the Apostolic Fathers—approximately AD 100;
>
> 2) Smyrna—Period of Persecution—AD 100 to approximately AD 313;
>
> 3) Pergamum—Rise of Heresies and Controversies—AD 313 to approximately AD 500;
>
> 4) Thyatira—First Pope/Rise of Islam to the Church Split (East and West)—AD 500 to approximately AD 1054;
>
> 5) Sardis—Rise of Moslem Latin Avveroism, Scholasticism, Monasticism, Crusades though the Middle Ages (Medieval Period)—1054 to approximately 1517;
>
> 6) Philadelphia—Protestant Reformation, Bible type-printed and translated, Revivals, Great Awakenings, Missionaries sent forth to rise of the Post-Modern Period—1517 to approximately 1960; and
>
> 7) Laodicea—Post-Modern Church (lukewarm, rich, with no need of anything, but really wretched, poor, blind, and naked, love grows cold, falling away, deceiving spirits [Jude 11–13, 18–19; 1 Tim 4:1; 2 Tim 3:1; 2 Thess 2:3–4; Rev 3:20]), last period before the end of the Church Age and Jesus, who is standing at the door, returns for His Body—1960 to the Rapture of the Church.[47]

Then, this kingdom concept will be consummated after the *Parousia* with the physical, literal, Millennial Kingdom on earth (Rev 20:1–9). Another subsequent chapter (chap. 6) is devoted entirely to the Millennium, where this all will be addressed in detail. However, related to this Kingdom of Heaven/God concept are the covenants God made with humanity throughout Biblical History.

The first recognizable covenant in the Bible is between God (*Yahweh*) and Abram, later changed by *Yahweh* to Abraham (Gen 17:1–5), contained in Genesis 12, 15, 17, and 18:1–22 (ca. 2,000 BC). However, the concept of covenant was already prevalent in the Ancient near East region (the Fertile Crescent), specifically the sub-region of Syria-Palestine (land of Canaan) in which Abraham lived.[48] At this time in the region, there were many tribes and kingdoms that fought over land and its natural resources. To coexist, they would establish alliances or treaties through the concept of covenant.[49] These treaties followed a set pattern, usually containing seven specific elements, including: stipulations, a list of witnesses, blessings and curses (rewards/punishments, which could include death), and a "ratification ceremony" (usually involving a blood sacrifice).[50] These treaties became known as "cutting covenant"[51] or blood covenant in this context. The terminology apparently served two purposes: 1) to symbolize the sealing or binding of the covenant between the two parties (from the Akkadian word *biritu*, meaning, "to fetter"); and 2) to communicate the potential consequences of breaking the covenant.[52]

Thus, the Hebraic Old Testament understanding of covenant comes from this history, and is rendered *berit* in Hebrew. The derivation of the word comes from several concepts: "to cut," "to eat," and "to fetter or bind together."[53] Yet, it goes deeper than that. A covenant establishes a relationship, since it creates "ties that bind."[54] A covenant is so binding and exclusive that in the Hebrew Bible, husbands and wives were married under covenants,[55] and the marriage covenant is the consecration of the two parties. In other words, the covenant makes the two parties holy and set apart, for each other to be "as one flesh" (Gen 2:24; Matt 19:5).[56]

Returning to the Abrahamic Covenant, Abraham was from the lineage of Shem (Semites, the chosen people of God—Gen 9:26–27; 11:10–26), and the first person called a "Hebrew" in the Bible (Gen 14:13). God's covenant with Abraham was a literal, eternal, unconditional, and unilateral (I will), blood covenant made with His covenant people (Hebrews, Israelites, Jews) of blessing which He would accomplish. It specifically involved:

> _Land_ (Canaan/Palestine—physically/geographically described by Gen 15:18–21, Num 34, Ezek 47:13–20—from the Euphrates River to the Wadi [River] of Egypt);
> _Seed_ (descendent, prophesied as the "Seed of the Woman," continuing with the miracle birth of Isaac, and culminating with the virgin birth of Messiah Jesus—Gen 3:15; 17; Rom 9:6–9; Gal 3:15–16); and
> _Blessing_ (spiritually—promise of redemption by grace through faith to all nations—Gen 12:3; 22:18; with Abraham as the Father of the righteous and faithful—Rom 4).[57]

The Abrahamic Covenant was then foundational and prototypical for all subsequent biblical covenants made. Other covenants that confirm the Abrahamic Covenant are the:

> 1) Mosaic Covenant (Exod 19–24)—though conditional/ temporal/bilateral, confirms "land, seed, and blessing";[58]
>
> 2) Palestinian Covenant (Deut 30:3–5)—although an extension of Mosaic Covenant, confirms only "land";[59]
>
> 3) Davidic Covenant (2 Sam 7:11–16)—though also eternal and unconditional, confirms only royal "seed"/spiritual "blessing" (King/Messiah Jesus);[60] and

4) <u>New Covenant</u> (Jer 31:31–40)—though also eternal and unconditional, confirms only relational, spiritual "blessing" (Messiah Jesus). It should be noted that although the title of "New Covenant" is used to describe the relational covenant that Christians have with God through Jesus Christ, this New Covenant in Jeremiah was given to the Israelites (to fulfill the spiritual component of the Abrahamic Covenant and may more correctly be called a "Renewed Covenant").[61]

This then is a perfect segue to Dispensationalism, Covenant Theology, and Replacement Theology.

Dispensationalism is a theological belief attributed to John Nelson (J. N.) Darby (1800–1882). Yet, many of its concepts predate Darby in the writings of Pierre Poiret (1687), John Edwards (1699), and Isaac Watts (1674–1748).[62] Generally speaking, it states that God deals with humanity throughout biblical history in a number of periods (usually seven) of time, economies, administrations, or *dispensations* (i.e., *Innocence*—the Garden of Eden before the Fall; *Conscience*—Adam to the Flood in Noah's day; *Government*—Post-Flood to Abraham; *Patriarchal Rule*—Abraham to Moses; *Mosaic Law*; *Grace or the Church Age*; and the *Millennial Kingdom*). Traditionally, all dispensationalists hold to the following four major doctrines:

1) A *distinct separation between an earthly Israel and the heavenly Church*;

2) A *clear separation between Old Covenant Law and New Covenant Grace*;

3) The New Testament Church is a *parenthesis* in God's plan, and was not foretold in the Old Testament; and

4) A *clear distinction between the Rapture of the Church and the Second Coming of Christ, separated by the Seven-year Tribulation.*

And, all of their beliefs are based on a literal, plenary interpretation of the Bible.[63]

There are three types of modern Dispensationalism: Scofieldian (named after Cyrus Ingerson [C. I.] Scofield [1843–1921]), Revised, and Progressive. Scofieldian Dispensationalism rigidly separates Israel and the Church. Revised Dispensationalism allows for more continuity between Israel and the Church, and between the various dispensations. And Progressive Dispensationalism is even more moderate, and sees considerable continuity in God's plan for humanity and avoids wild prophetic speculations.[64]

Covenant Theology is related to, but different from, Dispensationalism. It believes in only two dispensations (called covenants) that God made with humanity—Works and Grace. According to this theology, God made the Covenant of Works with Adam *before* the Fall—obey God and there is life; disobey God and there is death. Following the Fall, God instituted the Covenant of Grace—addressed and promised in Genesis 3:15, further outlined in the Old Testament, and pointing towards the Atonement in Jesus Christ (and explicitly outlined by the New Testament). The beginnings of this theology started Post-Reformation, and it was systematically addressed by Johannes Cocceius in 1648.[65]

Replacement Theology then takes Covenant Theology one step further. It basically states that the Church (addressed by the New Testament's New Covenant) replaces the nation of Israel (addressed by the Old Testament's Old Covenant) as God's chosen people in God's purposes and plans. Another name for Replacement Theology is Supersessionism—the Church *supersedes* the nation of Israel.[66]

All this being said by modern theology, and strictly speaking, I am not a dispensationalist, nor a Covenant/Replacement theologian. This is because I believe that the New Covenant (or Renewed Covenant) in Jesus Christ is a partial fulfillment of all the Abrahamic/Mosaic/Davidic Covenants *from the seed and spiritual blessing perspectives*, but not the *physical land perspective*. The Church seems to be foreshadowed in the Old Testament as Israel and is the spiritual fulfillment of spiritual Israel. Additionally, Jesus Christ was born a Jew in Israel, as a fulfillment of all the Old Testament messianic prophecies, and became the bridge between Old Testament Law, which He came to fulfill (Matt 5:17–18; Luke 16:16–17) and New Testament grace, which is exhibited by His Body, the Church. And finally, all the covenants are accessed by grace (in the Old Testament represented by the Hebrew word *chesed*, meaning "lovingkindness," or "covenant love")[67] through the same concept—faith (Rom 4:1–5:1).

Thus, the eschatological/teleological implications of the eternal nature of covenant and kingdom with the nation of Israel are:

> 1) Nation and Land forever—Israel became a nation again in 1948, but has continued to struggle with Arab neighbors over land/establishment of PLO/Palestinian State, and has yet to reclaim their full Abrahamic land inheritance;
>
> 2) King, Throne, and Kingdom forever—Messiah/King Jesus came nearly 2,000 years ago as the "Suffering Servant," of Isaiah 52–53, and introduced the Kingdom of Heaven/God, but not fully yet (until the *Parousia* and Millennial Reign); and
>
> 3) New Covenant, with blessings forever—Fulfilled in Messiah Jesus at His First Coming; but the Nation of Israel rejected Him as Messiah (Matt 21:42–45; 23:37–39; 27:20–26; Rom 9–11), but will repent and receive Him at His *Parousia*.

And therefore, all the covenants and the Kingdom of Heaven/God look toward a future completion in Messiah Jesus' *Parousia*. Thus in the next chapter, the Second Coming/Advent (*Parousia*) of Jesus Christ will be discussed in greater detail.

5.

The Second Coming of Jesus Christ

What Is the *Parousia*?

Jesus Christ's First Coming is confirmed in the New Testament by His fulfilling about eighty Old Testament prophecies concerning the Messiah (over many of which, He had no control). Some of these Old Testament scriptures are listed below, with their corresponding New Testament fulfillments:

Messianic Prophecy	OT Reference	NT Fulfillment
Son of God	Ps 2:7	Acts 13:33; Heb 1:5; 5:5
Son of Man	Dan 7:13	Matt 9:6; 12:8, 32, 40; 16:13
Incarnation	Ps 40:6–8	Heb 10:5–9
Virgin Birth	Isa 7:14	Matt 1:21–23
Born in Bethlehem	Mic 5:2	Matt 2:6; John 7:42
Lineage of Judah	Gen 49:10	Luke 3:23, 32
Lineage of David	2 Sam 7:12; Ps 110:1; Isa 11:1	Matt 22:43–44; John 7:42

Messianic Prophecy	OT Reference	NT Fulfillment
Flight to Egypt	Hos 11:1	Matt 2:15
Death of Babies by Herod	Jer 31:15	Matt 2:16–18
Anointing/Baptism	Isa 11:1–4; 61:1–3	Luke 3:21–22; 4:16–21
Use of Parables	Ps 78:2	Matt 13:35
Miracles	Isa 32:3–4; 35:5–6; 42:7	Matt 9:35; 11:4–5
Cleansing of the Temple	Ps 69:9	John 2:17
Triumphal Entry	Zech 9:9	Matt 21:5; John 12:14–15
The Arrest	Zech 13:7	Matt 26:54–56
The Scourging	Isa 53:5	John 19:1; 1 Pet 2:24–25
Casting Lots over Clothes	Ps 22:18	John 19:24
Bones not broken	Ps 34:20	John 19:36
Pierced side	Isa 53:5; Zech 12:10	John 19:37
Death	Deut 21:23; Ps 22; Isa 53; Dan 9:26	Luke 18:32; Acts 8:32–35; 1 Cor 15:3; Gal 3:13
Burial	Isa 53:9	John 19:38–41
Resurrection	2 Sam 22:6–7; Ps 16:8–11; 30:3; 41:10; Isa 57:1; Hos 6:2	Luke 24:46; Acts 2:25–31; 1 Cor 15:4

Messianic Prophecy	OT Reference	NT Fulfillment
Ascension	Ps 2:7; 16:10–11; 24:7–10; 68:18; 110:1	Mark 16:19; John 20:16–17; Acts 1:9–11; Eph 4:4
Second Covenant	Jer 31:31; Ezek 36:26	Matt 5:17; 26:26–28; John5: 43; 10:10; 1 Cor 11:23–26.[1]

From the scriptures outlined above and the content of the previous chapters, it may be seen that the Old Testament was written as a record of salvation acts for God's chosen people, as well as a foretelling of the coming of the ultimate "Salvation Act" of Messiah. As has been mentioned above, it has been commonly said within the Body of Christ that the history of the world is really "His-story" of Jesus Christ (*Yeshua Ha Mashiach*). This then includes both of His Comings (the Perfect/Complete Gospel of Phil 1:6) and both Old Testament prophetic-historical concepts of this Present Age and the Age to Come (*olam habbah*).

Jesus' First Coming was also confirmed by the historical record of respected Jewish and Roman historians of the time (e.g., Flavius Josephus, Tacitus, Pliny the Younger). Thus, all the events surrounding the life of Jesus Christ at His First Coming are undeniable, historical facts.[2] And by using the same Old and New Testament scriptures (some in Jesus' own words), we may determine that all the prophecies regarding Jesus' Second Coming will also come to pass in the historical future. With that in mind as a foundational thought, let us pursue the biblical understanding of this concept by first looking at the Greek New Testament words for "coming" or "advent."

In New Testament Greek, the English word "coming" is mainly

represented by two words: *erchomai* and *parousia*. The word *erchomai* means:

> to come, to go, move or pass along…in any direction…however, more frequently signifies—to come…in a future sense…but only of what is certain to take place (John 4:25; 14:3, 30; Rev 1:7)…the One who was (or had been) and the coming One (Rev 1:4, 8; 4:8)…*epi*, upon, implying rest upon (Matt 24:30—upon the clouds)…in the sense of to come again, back, to return…two of its many derivatives; *eleusis*, advent, coming; *katerchomai*, to come down.[3]

The Greek word *erchomenon*, the noun form of *erchomai*, is also translated "coming or arrival."[4]

The word *parousia* means, "present, presence, a being present, a coming to a place; presence, coming or arrival…*a technical term used of the Second Coming of Christ* (Matt 24:3; 1 Cor 15:23; 1 Thess 2:19; 2 Thess 2:8; 2 Pet 3:4; 1 John 2:28); *the Son of Man* (Matt 24:27, 37, 39); *the Lord* [emphasis added] (1 Thess 3:13; 4:15; 5:23; 2 Thess 2:1; James 5:7–8; 2 Pet 1:16); the day of God (2 Pet 3:12)." While the term *parousia* most commonly refers to the Second Coming of the Lord Jesus Christ, *this Parousia is not just one event taking place at a particular time; rather, it is made up of a series of events.* We can understand which event is referred to only by a careful examination of the scriptural context in which the words *parousia* or *erchomai* occur. For example, the *coming* of the Lord at the end of the Seven-year Tribulation Period is what the Lord describes in Matthew 24:15–22, 32–34; Mark 13:14–23, 29–30 (see also, Luke 19:41–44; 21:20–23, 32–33; 23:28–30). The judgment of the Lord associated with this *coming* is designated as a specific *coming* by the verb *elthe* (related to *erchomai*), indicating that this specific coming is prior to the final judgment of the world. This coming is also called an *apokalupsis*, "revelation" (Rom 2:5; 8:19; 1 Cor 1:7; 1 Pet 1:7,

13; 4:13), and an *epiphaneia*, "manifestation" (2 Thess 2:8; 1 Tim 6:14; 2 Tim 1:10; 4:1, 8; Titus 2:13). Thus, *"the coming of the Lord or His Parousia consists of several comings which are in reality stages of a continuous process* [emphasis added]."[5]

Another term that relates to the *Parousia* is *maranatha*. This word is a Greek transliteration of two Aramaic words: *maran,* meaning, "lord"; and *atha,* meaning, "has come." The only place that the word appears in the Bible is in 1 Corinthians 16:22. However, it is alluded to in Revelation 22:20 and mentioned in the mid-second century AD Christian writing *The Teaching of the Twelve Apostles* (*The Didache*) 10:6. In *The Didache,* the word *maranatha* is translated as "the Lord cometh or the Lord is come," as a reminder of the *Parousia* in a Communion (Lord's Supper, Eucharist) prayer (see 1 Cor 11:26).[6] Other definitions for *maranatha* are as follows: "our Lord has come," indicating the approaching judgment when the Lord returns;[7] "our Lord, come!"—see Revelation 22:20,[8] 2 Thessalonians 1:8–9 and Jude 14–16 for judgment on unbelievers, 2 Peter 2:9 for day of judgment, Revelation 1:3; 22:7, 12, 20 for "Lord, come quickly," Acts 1:11, Matthew 16:27, Daniel 7:13, Zechariah 14:5 for "come in like manner," and Philippians 4:5, 2 Timothy 4:8, Revelation 1:3 for "the Lord is at hand."[9] Considering all this information, it appears that *maranatha* is an exclamatory statement used by the Apostles as an encouragement to the Early Church; meaning, Lord Jesus, come, which specifically refers to the *Parousia*. Therefore, when addressing all the terms related to the Second Coming or Advent of Christ and all events related to it, *Parousia* is the most commonly used word to describe all that they entail, and will be used from this point forward to convey that concept.

The key to separating the two eschatological comings of the Messiah in the Old Testament prophecies is in the differing purpose for each coming. The First Coming involves the suffering servant of Isaiah 52–53 for the atonement of the sin of humanity and reconciling or restoring relationship with *Yahweh*. The Second Coming (*Parousia*) involves the glorious King of Kings and Lord of Lords of Revelation 19 coming: to complete the salvation of His beloved Body (the Church) through physical resurrection and rapture (to be specifically dealt with in chapter 8), to judge the earth for its sins (Day of the LORD—chapter 7), and to set up His kingdom on earth for one thousand years (Millennium—chapter 6). Many of the Old Testament prophecies concerning the first coming of the Messiah for salvation also contain prophecies concerning the *Parousia* for judgment. There are also specific, separate prophecies concerning the Day of the Lord (or Day of *Yahweh*) in regards to judgment (chapter 7). Finally, the Old Testament contains separate promises of hope and restoration of the kingdom for *Yahweh*'s chosen people on earth in the Millennium (chapter 6).

Just as the first four Old Testament annual feasts—Passover, Unleavened Bread, First Fruits, and Weeks (or Pentecost)—were fulfilled at Jesus' First Coming, all of these types of prophecies surrounding the *Parousia* of Jesus are seen in the prophetic eschatological fulfillment of the last three Old Testament annual feasts—Trumpets, Atonement, and Booths (or Tabernacles), **separated by a "gap," called the Times of the Gentiles or the Church Age** (see chapter 3 above for specific delineation of this). Next, the specific prophecies related to the *Parousia* will be addressed.

Two of the *Parousia* prophecies were highlighted by Justin Martyr (AD 100–165) in his *Dialogue with Trypho, a Jew*. In roughly half of this document, Justin tries to prove that Jesus Christ was the Messiah that the Jews were anticipating. He addresses "Elijah coming first" in Malachi 3:1 and 4:5 as two separate comings/advents. Malachi 3:1, corresponding to Isaiah

40:1–17, speaks about John the Baptist (confirmed by Jesus Himself in Matt 11:7–11; 17:10–13). Malachi 4:5 speaks of another messenger (possibly one of the two witnesses mentioned in Rev 11:3–12) coming prior to the *Parousia*. Justin Martyr then continues on with the thought of the Messiah's two advents by quoting Genesis 49:8–12, Jacob's (Israel's) prophetic statement about Judah and his descendants. He points out that the "scepter or ruler's staff (kingship) will not depart until Shiloh comes." Then, "He ties the foal to the vine and donkey's colt to the choice vine and washes his garments in wine and his robes in the blood of grapes." He goes on to explain that Jesus is Shiloh, the last king, and there will be no more Old Testament-type kings until the Second Advent. The Gentiles are the foal, accepting Jesus as the Christ. Jesus came as a donkey's colt without the yoke of the Law, as symbolized by His riding a donkey's colt into Jerusalem (prophesied by Zech 9:9). The dipping of garments in wine and the "blood" of grapes signifies Jesus' blood shed to cleanse believers. Therefore, Jesus fulfilled the Messiah's First Coming and the related prophecies. Justin Martyr then adds that Psalm 110:1–4 speaks about Jesus and His thousand-year' reign as king, at His Second Coming. Thus, all the other prophecies about Messiah's Second Coming "show that He must be resurrected to come again a second time." He adds that even though Trypho, and the entire Nation of Israel for that matter, missed Jesus' First Coming as Messiah, they will have an opportunity at His Second Coming to accept Him as Messiah for the first time.[10]

William E. Biederwolf, in his *The Second Coming Bible Commentary* (1985), also outlines the following scriptures that speak of the *Parousia*. Genesis 24:63–67 relates the story of Isaac going out to meet his bride Rebekah, which portrays him as a type of Jesus meeting His bride, the Church, in the clouds in 1 Thessalonians 4:14–16.[11] Psalm 45:1–17 represents the union of Christ and the Church at His *Parousia*.[12] Psalms 93

– 99 show *Yahweh* as coming to judge the earth and reign as king; especially 94:1, 2, 23; 96:13; 97; and 98:9.[13] Psalm 110 speaks of the Messiah as a "priest forever according to the order of Melchizedek" (Heb 5:6, 10; 6:20; 7:17, 21); judging the nations, filling them with corpses and ruling.[14] Isaiah 9:6–7 speaks of both of Messiah's advents: His First Advent at birth in verse 6 and the *Parousia* as king and ruler on the throne of David in verse 7.[15] Isaiah 61:1–11 also speaks of both advents: verses 1 to the middle of 2 address the First Advent (Luke 4:17–21); and from there to the end addresses the *Parousia*.[16] Isaiah 66:15–24 speaks of *Yahweh* coming in fire and in chariots like the whirlwind to judge the nations.[17] Daniel 2:34 tells of "a stone was cut out without hands," and it struck Nebuchadnezzar's statue on its feet of iron and clay, and crushed them. This represents Jesus' Second Coming, when He will judge the kingdoms of this world and set up His Kingdom.[18] Daniel 7:13–14 states, "One like a Son of Man coming" to set up His kingdom on the earth.[19] In Micah 5:2–15, verses 2–3 speak of Messiah's First Advent and birth in Bethlehem; while verses 4–15 speak of the Second Advent with Messiah ruling, reigning, and judging.[20] Zechariah 14:3–21 speaks of Messiah coming with "all the holy ones with him"; after which, He will literally "stand on the Mount of Olives" to judge the nations and set up His Kingdom on earth.[21] Finally, Malachi 3:1–6 speaks of the First Advent and John the Baptist, and Malachi 4:1–4 speaks of the Second Advent and "Elijah the prophet" preceding it.[22]

J.R. Church, in his book *Hidden Prophecies in the Psalms* (1986), agrees with the eschatological nature and prophetic voice of certain psalms that speak of the events surrounding the *Parousia*. Psalm 2 predicts the battles of Gog, Magog, and Armageddon before the Messiah's Second Advent to rule His Millennial Kingdom.[23] Psalm 24 predicts the return of the Messiah at the Battle of Armageddon.[24] Psalm 48 predicts the restoration of the Nation of Israel in 1948, and the beginning of what Jewish scholars predicted would be "'Messianic times'—that special generation which is preparing the world for the coming of Messiah to establish the promised 'kingdom of heaven' on earth."[25] Psalm 83 predicts the Arab nations coming against, and trying to destroy, Israel. But it also notes that they will ultimately be destroyed at the Battle of Armageddon, when Christ shall return to earth with His Bride (the Church) and set up the Millennial Kingdom.[26] Psalm 85 predicts the rebuilding of the Temple (including the return of the Ark of the Covenant), which will signal the beginning of Daniel's "seventieth week" (the Rapture of the Church, rise of the Antichrist and the Tribulation), culminating with the Battle of Armageddon and the *Parousia*.[27] Church adds, "Psalms 88–94…describe the future seven years of Jacob's trouble in chronological order."[28] Psalm 94, in particular, is the culmination of these seven years, and predicts the "day of vengeance," or Armageddon, and the glorious Second Coming of Jesus.[29] Then, Psalm 110 "declares the coming of Christ to establish His Kingdom. Verse 1 refers to the past 2,000 years between His First Coming and His Second Coming…. The following verses declare His glorious return: (vv. 2, 4–6)."[30] And finally, Psalm 144:5 is "a prayer for the personal appearing of the Messiah."[31]

Additionally, the following eschatological information is provided on Psalms 2 and 126. Psalm 2 is a prayer for the eschatological victory of God and His Messiah, or the "time when God's kingdom and the kingdom of this world will be identical."[32] And, "Psalm 126 is a prophetic song that takes the exiles' joy of their returning to their homeland and looks towards the future of Zion and in doing so makes a multiple metaphoric reference to the advent of the Lord when he will bring the final restoration and salvation."[33]

From the different testimonies above, which show the Old

Testament scriptures that speak of the *Parousia* of Jesus Christ (especially the verses that contain eschatological prophecies of both comings of the Messiah), it may be concluded that the Perfect/Complete Gospel of Both Comings of Jesus Christ is a, if not the, major theme of the Old Testament. Next, the New Testament scriptures addressing the *Parousia* will be addressed, starting with Jesus' very own words regarding it.

The concept of the *Parousia* was first separated from the First Advent by Jesus Himself and taught as such, even though both comings/advents of Messiah were addressed distinctly by the Old Testament (see above). Most of Jesus' teachings are focused on concepts related to the Kingdom of Heaven/God (e.g., the Kingdom Parables, the Sermon on the Mount, the Lord's Prayer, the Olivet or Apocalyptic Discourse, the Words of Institution at the Last Supper, and the Great Commission—see chapter 4 above). Some of the *Parousia* teachings of Jesus overlap with the kingdom teachings (e.g., Matt 10:23; 16:27–28; 25; Luke 17:20–37), while others stand alone and are mostly included in the Olivet or Apocalyptic Discourse (Matt 24; Mark 13; Luke 17 and 21). These passages relate to the future final victory of the kingdom of God over the kingdom of this world per Revelation 11:15.[34] Although there are other references made by Jesus of His *Parousia* (e.g., John 14:2–3; 21:22–23), and even references made by His actions (the triumphal entry into Jerusalem on a donkey on Palm Sunday as told in Luke 19:28–44),[35] the bulk of His teaching on the subject is contained in the Apocalyptic Discourse. And, it is that which will now be addressed. Although the Greek word *parousia* is only used in Matthew's account of the Apocalyptic Discourse, the same concept carries through to the other two accounts. Consider Matthew's use of *parousia* in the following examination of his Gospel account.

The Gospel of Matthew (probably written in the AD 60s) was set in an Old Testament prophetic time context. It was written with a Jewish audience in mind, from a Jewish perspective, and most probably by the converted Jewish tax collector, the Apostle Matthew/Levi himself.[36] In fact, according to the Early Church Apostolic Father Papias (ca. AD 70–163), it was probably written originally in Hebrew and later in Greek.[37] The Hebrew word for "coming" used in Matthew 24 is *bow*, meaning, "to go or come, bring." Although different forms of this word are used in Matthew 24, the same meaning is applied to all usages.[38] However, the usage in verse 30, "the Son of Man coming on the clouds of the sky with power and great glory," is a specific reference back to Daniel 7:13, which was written in Aramaic. The Aramaic word *athah*, meaning, "to arrive: come, bring" was used by Daniel in that verse.[39] The word used for *athah* in the Septuagint (the Greek version of the Old Testament) is *erchomenos* (a form of *erchomai*).[40] This Hebraic text and usage of the word will now be compared to the Greek text where two separate words are used (*parousia* and *erchomai*).

Previous to this section of scripture (in Matthew 23), Jesus was talking to the Pharisees about the Kingdom of Heaven/God and the future of Jerusalem while at the Temple. He concludes in verse 39: "For I say to you, from now on you shall not see Me until you say, 'Blessed is He who comes (*erchomai*) in the name of the Lord!'" Apparently, this is a statement about the Nation of Israel not accepting Jesus as the Messiah until His Second Coming.[41] Next in Matthew 24:1–2, Jesus came out of the Temple. And after the disciples had pointed out the Temple buildings to Him, He said, "Do you not see all these things? Truly I say to you, not one stone here shall be left upon another, which will not be torn down." We now know that Jesus was prophesying about the destruction of the city of Jerusalem and the Temple by the Romans in AD 70 (fulfilled some forty years after He made that prophetic declaration)!

The first use of the word *parousia* is found in verse 3, where the disciples ask three questions: "Tell us, when will these things be, and what will be the sign of Your coming (*Parousia*), and of the end of the age?" Please note that the context of the questions clearly points to the events surrounding the Old Testament prophecies of the Day of the Lord and the Messiah establishing His kingdom on earth. This is evidenced by a similar question from the disciples just prior to Jesus' ascension in Acts 1:6: "Is it at this time You are restoring the kingdom to Israel?" Matthew's account alone contains three questions, the other two accounts (Mark 13 and Luke 21) only two, thereby excluding the question about Jesus' *Parousia*. And, since Matthew alone uses *parousia* in the text, he was the only one of the three Gospel writers of this Apocalyptic Discourse to be present as an eye-witness, he uses *erchomai* in other places in this text, and he had no concept of the Church as the new theocratic nation of God's plan, *parousia* in this text probably refers to Jesus' coming for His own holy people (the holy Jews or the restored Jewish nation referred to in Daniel 12:1).

Jesus then proceeds to answer their questions, starting in verse 4 (from a Jewish believer's perspective in prophetic time, looking forward to apocalyptic time). He chronicles the first 3½ year period of the Tribulation through verse 14, and then, speaks of the Abomination of Desolation (spoken of in Dan 9:27; 12:11) in verse 15. This becomes the dividing point of the Tribulation Period and starts the Great Tribulation (last 3½ years, as mentioned in verse 21).

Jesus then shifts to answering the question about His future coming in Matthew 24:23 by warning them not to be misled by false "christs" and false prophets. In verse 25, He emphasizes this point by saying, "Behold, I have told you in advance." He then goes on to describe His coming in verse 26 by saying what it will *not* be (based on any human knowledge, wisdom or origin). In verse 27, He states what it *will* be (based on heavenly origin, like "lightning").

Verses 27–31 then describe His *Coming*. However, based on the Greek text there appear to be "two separate comings described," instead of two separate references to one coming. The first coming is contained in verse 27 using the word *parousia*. The exact same language is used in Luke 17:24, and is similar language to Paul's description of the Rapture of the Church in 1 Corinthians 15 ("just as lightning comes from the east, and flashes even to the west," compared to "in a moment, in the twinkling of an eye"). The second coming is addressed in verses 30 and 31, where the word *erchomenon*, or coming with "power and great glory" is used (as also described in Dan 7:13, in the Septuagint, Matt 16:27; Mark 13:26; Luke 21: 27; and Rev 19:11–16). These two distinct comings are separated by verses describing the Battle of Armageddon, the conclusion of the Tribulation, and Old Testament quotes about the "day of the LORD" (Isa 13:10; 34:4; Joel 2:10) and the "sign of the Son of Man" appearing in the sky. Then, associated with the *erchomenon* coming in verse 31, the angels will "gather together His elect from the four winds, from one end of the sky to the other."

So, taking into account the definition of the *Parousia* (above) and the fact that the Apocalyptic Discourse is answering the disciples' questions about the "end of the Age" (*eschaton*), the *Parousia* does seem to include all the events surrounding Jesus' Second Coming put into the language of a first-century Jewish believer. Next, Jesus' words in the Lord's Prayer, the Words of Institution, and the Great Commission will be examined for their references to the *Parousia*.

The Lord's Prayer (Matt 6:9–13; Luke 11:1–4) represents a pattern of prayer that Jesus taught His disciples. However, it has become a prayer itself in all Christendom, especially in the more liturgical denominations (e.g., Roman Catholicism and Anglicanism). The mentioning of "Thy kingdom come" and "Thine is the kingdom, and the power, and the glory, forever. Amen," speaks of the Kingdom of Heaven/God by Jesus. This phrase also addresses the fact that this kingdom truly belongs to God; that it is a teleological kingdom (not fully here yet, but will come); that the believer gives up allegiance to the kingdom of this world and yields to God's Kingdom; and that this is the Kingdom that is the inheritance of the Perfect/Complete Gospel of Jesus Christ.[42]

At the Last Supper, Jesus gave what has come to be known as His Words of Institution to establish the New Covenant in His blood during the Jewish Feast of Passover (Matt 26:26–29; Mark 14:22–25; Luke 22:15–20; 1 Cor 5:7–8). Additionally, these words establish a means for believers to remember and fellowship with Him as the Body of Christ (Holy Communion/ Lord's Supper/Eucharist) throughout the Church Age, until His *Parousia* and the coming of His future kingdom.[43] *The teleological nature of Holy Communion* is addressed by Paul in 1 Corinthians 11:23–26: "For as often as you eat this bread and drink the cup, you proclaim the Lord's death *until He comes* [emphasis added]." Remembering what Jesus did for His Body through the table fellowship, or feast of Holy Communion, looks to the past of Jesus' sacrificial act at His crucifixion nearly two thousand years ago, brings that great act of the Atonement into the present, and generates hope for the future *Parousia* of Christ (when the marriage supper of the Lamb of Revelation 19:9 will be held). Therefore, "For that reason, commemorating Christ leads on the call of expectation, *maranatha*! (*Didache* 10:6; cf. 1 Cor 16:22). In that cry, the proclamation of the death of Christ reaches its intended purpose."[44] This expectation and exclamation of hope has been made part of modern orthodox liturgical services in the prayer of thanksgiving (or declaration of the "Mystery of the Faith"): "Christ has died, Christ has risen, and Christ will come again."[45]

Finally, the Great Commission of Jesus, given to His disciples (Matt 28:18–20; Mark 16:15–16; Luke 24:47–49; Acts 1:6–11), and by extension of the High Priestly Prayer of John 17:20, to the successive generations of disciples, speaks in teleological tones also. Jesus was clear that the Great Commission was to last "even to the end of the age" and until His coming again. This is confirmed by the answer to the question the disciples asked in Acts 1:6, about "restoring the kingdom to Israel" at that time. Jesus redirected their attention to the mission of the Church Age, which was to "be My witnesses both in Jerusalem, and in all Judea and Samaria, and even to the remotest part of the earth" through the power (*dunamis*) of the Holy Spirit (Acts 1:8). Then, Jesus gave His disciples (present there in Acts and throughout the entire Church Age) hope of the Rapture of the Church and His *Parousia* by His physical and visible *ascension* (*rapture*) into heaven (Acts 1:9–11). See chapter 8 for a more complete development of Jesus' ascension as a precursory type of the Rapture of the Church.

Included as part of the Great Commission are the following words: "...baptizing them in the name of the Father and the Son and the Holy Spirit." This not only speaks of the importance of water baptism as part of the conversion experience/becoming a citizen of the kingdom of God,[46] but it also connects the sacrament, covenantal sign, or ordinance of Baptism, with the Perfect/Complete Gospel and the Body of Christ.[47] One may conclude that the above statements made by Jesus in these three foundational and fundamental areas of the Church (the Lord's Prayer, Holy Communion, and the Great Commission), are teleological in nature and tie directly into the Perfect/Complete Gospel of Both Comings of the Lord Jesus Christ (Phil 1:6).

The final section of Jesus' statements that testifies of the teleological nature of His Gospel are His references to being the "Author and Finisher," "Alpha and Omega," and "Beginning and End." Author and Finisher (Perfecter) is not a name used by Jesus Himself, but is a name assigned to Jesus by the writer of Hebrews in 12:2. It is also addressed by Paul in Philippians 1:6: "He who *began a good work in you will perfect it* until the day of Jesus Christ" [emphasis added]. This name connects Jesus not only to the beginning and completion of salvation (*Perfect/ Complete Gospel encapsulated*), but also to the beginning and the consummation of the Church Age. This concept is further confirmed by the words of Jesus about Himself in Revelation 21:6 and 22:13, "I am the Alpha and Omega, the beginning and the end," and as part of the Triune Godhead in Revelation 1:8, "I am the Alpha and the Omega, says the Lord God, 'who is and who was and who is to come, the Almighty.'" These statements, contained in the last book of the Bible, connect (show the continuity, "scarlet thread," of the "whole counsel" of God's Word) not only the God of the Old Testament (as addressed in Isa 41:4; 44:6; and 48:12 as the "First and the Last") with the God of the New Testament, but the salvation of God from the Old Testament to the New Testament ("by grace through faith") by the vision of the Perfect/Complete Gospel in the person of Jesus Christ.

Again, throughout the entire New Testament, just as in the Old Testament, the theme of Jesus as the teleological Messiah/ Savior/Lord is intertwined. According to Oral Roberts, specifically, this is addressed as follows: the Messiah in Matthew, the Wonderworker in Mark, the Son of Man in Luke, the Son of God in John, the Holy Spirit working among men in Acts, the Justifier in Romans, the Sanctifier in 1 and 2 Corinthians, the Redeemer from the curse of the Law in Galatians, the unsearchable riches in Ephesians, the Supplier of needs in Philippians, the fullness of God in bodily form in

Colossians, the soon coming King in 1 and 2 Thessalonians, the Mediator between God and humanity in 1 and 2 Timothy, the Faithful Pastor in Titus, the Friend of the oppressed in Philemon, the blood of the everlasting covenant in Hebrews, the Lord who raises the sick in James, the Chief Shepherd who will soon appear in 1 and 2 Peter, love in 1–3 John, the coming Lord with ten thousand of His saints in Jude, and the King of Kings and Lord of Lords in Revelation.[48] In addition to the accounts of Jesus' teachings on the Perfect/Complete Gospel contained in the Gospels addressed above, the New Testament contains other written material by an assortment of writers—Luke, Paul, the writer of Hebrews, James, Peter, Jude, and John.

Luke, as a disciple of Paul and Early Church historian, addresses the Perfect/Complete Gospel in Acts 2:14–47; 3:13–26; 7:1–53; 13:32–47; 15:1–21; and 28:23–27[49] and in his gospel account of the "Triumphal Entry" into Jerusalem in Luke 19:28–44.[50] Paul (who saw the heavenly Jesus in a vision on the road to Damascus in Acts 9, and also possibly when he was raptured to "paradise" in 2 Cor 12:2–4) was appointed the Apostle to the Gentiles by Jesus and became the most prolific writer on the Perfect/Complete Gospel.[51] This appears most evident in the following passages: Romans 2:1–16; 4–5; 8:1–30; 9–11; 13:11–14; 14:8–12; 15:8–13; 1 Corinthians 10:1–11; 11:23–26; 15; 2 Corinthians 12:1–4; Galatians 3:1–4:7; Ephesians 1:11–2:7; 3:4–13; 5:27; 6:10–20; Philippians 1:3–6, 10; Col 1; 1 Thessalonians 1:10; 2:19–20; 3:13; 4:13–5:24; 2 Thessalonians 1:5–2:14; 1 Timothy 4:1–5; 2 Timothy 1:8–12; 2:8–13; 3:1–9; 4:1–8; and Titus 2:11–14; 3:5–7.[52] This may be summed up best by Paul's writings in Philippians 1:6: "For I am sure that God, *who began the good work within you, will continue his work until it is finally finished* (*teleios*) [emphasis added] on that day when Christ Jesus comes back again" (NLT), and Titus 2: 11–13: "For the *grace of God has appeared, bringing salvation to all men*…and to live sensibly, righteously, and godly in the present age, looking for the *blessed hope and the appearing of the glory of our great God and Savior, Christ Jesus*" [emphasis added].

The writer of Hebrews corroborates the Perfect/Complete Gospel in Hebrews 9:12–28 and 10:37–12:2, 26–7.[53] James, a half-brother of Jesus and leader of the Jerusalem Church, addresses the Perfect/Complete Gospel in James 5:3, 7–9.[54] Peter, one of the closest three apostles to Jesus and the Apostle to the Jews, addresses the Perfect/Complete Gospel in 1 Peter 1:3–12; 2:4–10; 4:1–7; and 2 Peter 1:11, 16, 19; 3.[55] This is best summed up by 1 Peter 1:3–5, "Blessed be the God and Father of our Lord Jesus Christ, who according to His great mercy *has caused us to be born again to a living hope* through the resurrection of Jesus Christ from the dead, *to obtain an inheritance* which is imperishable and undefiled and will not fade away, *reserved in heaven for you*, who are protected by the power of God through faith *for a salvation ready to be revealed in the last time*" [emphasis added]. Jude, also a half-brother of Jesus, addresses the Perfect/Complete Gospel in verses 14–23.[56]

John was the closest apostle to Jesus and the one whom Jesus directed to care for His mother Mary (John 19:26–27). He also was the apostle who lived the longest and saw a vision of the teleological Jesus in all His glory in heaven while in exile on the Isle of Patmos (Rev 1). As a result, he may have been the most qualified, in addition to Paul, to address the Perfect/Complete Gospel of Jesus Christ. Aside from the several references to it in his Gospel (addressed above), John addresses it again more thoroughly in 1 John 2:14 – 3:3[57] and throughout the entire Book of Revelation.[58] John puts it succinctly in 1 John 3:2, "Beloved, *now we are children of God*, and it has not appeared as yet what we shall be. We know that, *when He appears, we shall be like Him, because we shall see Him just as He is*" [emphasis added]. Revelation is not only the last book written in the Bible and an apocalyptic view of the *eschaton* of time, but is an "unveiling," or clear picture, of the ever-living Word of God and center of the Perfect/Complete Gospel of Salvation, Atonement, and Restoration interwoven throughout the entire printed Word of God—*Yeshua HaMashiach*, the Lord Jesus Christ, God's Son, Savior, the Alpha and Omega, the Beginning and the End. A fitting conclusion to this writing on the *Parousia* of Jesus Christ is addressed by the phrase, "behold the Lamb" in Revelation 5:6, by speaking of Jesus as the beginning, end, and the way of the Perfect/Complete Gospel.[59] With this as an overarching and foundational understanding of the *Parousia*, the next chapter will begin considering the first of three main events or separate eschatological concepts contained therein: the Millennium.

6.

What Is the Millennium?

Although the Second Coming of Jesus is an accepted biblical and theological fact within Christendom (addressed by the previous chapter), *when* Jesus actually returns relative to the events of the *Parousia* (the Millennium, the Tribulation, the Rapture of the Church, and associated resurrections and judgments) remains very controversial. So first we must take time to address the different theological views of the Millennium. The concept of the Millennium is based on Old Testament prophecies about the Messiah establishing the Kingdom of Heaven/God on earth and the "already, not yet" view of the Kingdom outlined by Jesus Himself at His First Coming (see chapter 4). The Millennium is traditionally believed to be explained in the New Testament by the text in Revelation 20:1–10 (primarily, verses 1–6), which mentions six times a period of "one thousand years."

Therefore, a person's view of the *Parousia* is foundationally affected by one's understanding of the Millennium described in Revelation 20:1–10. The term "millennium" comes from the Latin words, *milus*, meaning thousand, and *annum*, meaning years—together meaning, a thousand years.[1] There are three basic views of the Millennium described below.

1) <u>Premillennial View</u>. This view is taken from the literal chronological reading of Revelation 4–20 (primarily 19:11–20:10). Please see chapter 2 regarding the literal "futurist" interpretation of the Book of Revelation. According

to this view, the Millennium occurs after the Seven-Year Tribulation, Armageddon, the Second Coming of Jesus, "the first resurrection," (Rev 20:5–6), and the Judgments of Israel and the Nations/Gentiles (Rev 19; Matt 24–25). Prior to the Millennium, Satan is bound and cast into "the bottomless pit," which is sealed for the duration of one thousand years (Rev 20:1–3). Then, Messiah Jesus reigns as King of Kings and Lord of Lords (and resurrected Saints reign with Him—Rev 20:4–6). The redeemed nation of Israel and the redeemed of the nations (Gentiles), who survived the Tribulation and judgments, will repopulate the earth. The Millennium lasts "literally" 1,000 years (which is the completion of the General Creation Week Prophetic Timeline of 7,000 years, mentioned in chapter 3). The Millennial Kingdom also includes the Millennial Temple (or Third Temple), per Ezekiel 37:15–28 and 40–46:24 (as a preview of the "New Jerusalem" of Rev 21). Thus, the Premillennial belief teaches that Jesus Christ will literally and bodily return to earth at the end of the Seven-year Tribulation (see the next chapter), instituting a literal and physical one thousand-year reign (the Millennium) of peace and prosperity on the earth.[2] Historically, the Church Fathers, up to and including the First Ecumenical Council at Nicaea in AD 325, were almost exclusively premillennialists. Their premillennial perspective did not begin to change until the time of Origen and his allegorical interpretation of Scripture in the late third century AD. And, it did not fully change until Augustine's Amillennial doctrine became the orthodox view of the Church in the early fifth century AD.[3]

The Millennial Kingdom fulfills all eternal Covenants mentioned in chapter 4 (Abrahamic, Davidic, and New). Specifically, this done in relation to:

1) the Land—the national borders per Gen 15:18–21; confirmed by Num 34:1–15 and Ezek 47:13–21;

2) the Seed—the Hebrews/Israelites/Jews that make up the nation of Israel; and

3) the King/Throne/Royal House and Spiritual Blessing—New Heart/forgiveness of Sin/filling of Holy Spirit.[4]

The Millennial Kingdom will then be characterized by "righteousness, obedience, holiness, truth, and fullness of the Holy Spirit," which includes: "peace, joy, holiness, glory, comfort, justice, full knowledge, instruction," wholeness, maturity, prosperity, "unified worship, and the manifest presence of God."[5] The government in the Millennium will be a Theocracy (over the fulfilled Kingdom of Heaven/God on earth, with Messiah/King Jesus ruling and reigning from Jerusalem). And, resurrected Saints will be reigning with King Jesus (e.g., Resurrected King David as Regent, Nobles, Governors, Lesser Authorities, and Judges), ruling over the redeemed Jews (which includes the restored nation of Israel—Rom 11:26–27) and redeemed Gentiles living at Jesus' Second Coming.[6] The study of this view, specifically called Premillennialism, is also known as Chiliasm, from the Greek word *chilioi* (also meaning thousand). The people who believe in this are also known as Millenarians or Chiliasts.[7]

Premillennialism is divided into two groups. Historicism believes that the prophecies concerning the End Times provide a symbolic history of the Church Age leading up to the *Parousia*. Their proponents examine past and present Church History to seek fulfillment of specific prophecies. On the other hand, Futurism believes that none of the End Times prophecies will be fulfilled until a short period before the *Parousia*. Futurism is further divided into three groups, based on their belief of when, and if, the Rapture (Catching Away) of the Church (see chapter 8) takes place: 1) Pretribulationalism—the Rapture takes place before the Seven-Year Tribulation; 2) Midtribulationalism—the Rapture takes place midway through the Tribulation; and 3)

<u>Posttribulationalism</u>—the <u>Rapture is not a separate event, and takes place in conjunction with the *Parousia*.</u>[8]

2) <u>Postmillennial View</u>. This view teaches that through the preaching of the Gospel by the Church and "the saving work of the Holy Spirit" during the Church Age, "the Kingdom of God is present on earth in the hearts of humanity" for an extended period of time, moving toward a worldwide time of peace and righteousness (*but not a literal 1,000 years*). Then, the end of this period (which is viewed as an allegorical fulfillment of the Millennium in Rev 20) will usher in the *Parousia*.[9] And thus, there will be no "literal" Millennium after the *Parousia*. This view may have started with Early Church Fathers Origen (ca. AD 185–254), Eusebius (ca. AD 263–339), and Athanasius (ca. AD 296–373).[10] It is also believed that during this time period, Tyconius (d. AD 390?) challenged the majority premillennial belief of the Early Church Fathers by saying the Millennium "refers to the present age." This view was later modified by Augustine and became the dominant view of the interpretation of Revelation 20 for "approximately the next thirteen centuries."[11] Then, Postmillennialism became popularized by the Puritans—by the influences of John Locke (1632–1704) and Daniel Whitby (1638–1726) in England,[12] and Jonathan Edwards (1703–1758) and the Great Awakening in the United States.[13]

3) <u>Amillennial View</u>. This view is taken from the prefix a-, meaning "no or none." This view also states that there is no "literal" Millennium (*again, an allegorical or "symbolic" interpretation of Rev 20*). And, all related prophecies are fulfilled during the period between the two comings of Jesus Christ (the Church Age). This view most likely originated with Origen (ca. AD 185–254), was endorsed by Church Fathers Eusebius (ca. AD 263–339) and Ambrose (ca. AD 340–4 April 397), and was adopted as the belief of the newly established

Roman Catholic Church by Augustine, Bishop of Hippo (AD 354–430) in the late-fourth century AD.[14] Amillennialism is very similar in belief to Postmillennialism, and was considered to be the official position of the Church from Augustine until the Protestant Reformation (and is still the position of the Roman Catholic and Eastern Orthodox Churches today). The Amillennialists also believe: that there is no literal reign of Christ on earth; that there is a general resurrection and judgment for all humanity immediately after Jesus' Second Coming; and then, all humanity (both believers and non-believers alike) is assigned to its eternal, final state (heaven or hell). However, one point of difference between Amillennialists and Postmillennialists is that Amillennialists do not believe in this period getting better and better with the spread of the Gospel and ending in a period of peace. They believe that Jesus could come back at any time, much like the Premillennialists.[15] Next, we will look at the history of these millennial views within Church History.

As stated above, historically, the Church Fathers, up to and including the First Ecumenical Council at Nicaea in AD 325, were almost exclusively premillennialists.[16] This testimony may best be summed up by the following statement: "With one exception [Caius] there is no Church Father before Origen who opposed the millenarian interpretation, and there is no one before Augustine whose extant writings offer a different interpretation of Revelation 20 than that of a future earthly kingdom consonant with the natural interpretation of the language."[17] However, after Augustine adopted Amillennialism, late in the fourth century AD, Premillennialism began to fade as the accepted view.[18] So much so, that by the time of the Third Ecumenical Council at Ephesus in AD 431, the Millennium was condemned as "superstitious."[19]

Following Augustine's declaration of Amillennialism as the

orthodox belief of the Church and the Council of Ephesus's statement against Premillennialism, there were only small groups of believers (usually common folk or peasants during times of social, political, or economic unrest) throughout the Middle Ages who held to Premillennialism.[20] However, this was fed by the circulation of the *Sibylline Oracles* (a compilation of 15 books of Greek female prophets predicting the future) coupled with John's Revelation and Joachim of Fiore's (ca. 1135–1202) view of three ages or dispensations of the world: 1) the Father (Law—Old Testament); the Son (grace—New Testament and Church Age); and the Holy Spirit (spiritual Church—the Millennium).[21]

Building on Joachim's Premillennialism and heading into the Reformation were the following groups: the Franciscan and Dominican monks, some of whom saw themselves as part of the 144,000 male virgins in Revelation 14;[22] Taborite Millenarians (taken from Mt. Tabor in Israel, believed to be the place from where Jesus ascended to heaven and to which He is to return at His Second Coming) from around Prague and radical followers of John Huss (1371–1415), who believed that purification of the land and revolt of the established State and Church were necessary to usher in the Second Coming and Millennium; Thomas Muntzer (1489–1525), known for starting the Peasant Revolts and Wars in Germany; Melchoir Hoffman (1495–1543), Anabaptist, and his "New Jerusalem teaching" in northern Germany and the Netherlands; and Menno Simons (1496–1561), leader of the Anabaptists in the Netherlands, who became later known as the Mennonites.[23] All of this culminated in four different millennial views coming out of the Reformation: 1) Augustine's Amillennialism; 2) Luther's postmillennial view that the Millennium had occurred in the past, and they were living in evil times awaiting divine intervention; 3) Calvin's postmillennial view that the Millennium will occur in the future, as the Elect gradually win the world for Christ, and then, the Second Advent will come; and 4) the Anabaptists' premillennial view.[24]

After the Reformation, a five-hundred page commentary on the Book of Revelation entitled *In Sacrum Beati Ioannis Apostoli, & Evangelistiae Apocalypsin Commentarij* (*The Mass of the Apostle St. John, and Evangelistic Commentary on Revelation*) was published by a Spanish-born Jesuit Priest named Francisco Ribera in 1590. In this work, he concluded that the antichrist would come in the future (beginnings of Premillennial Futurism) for a literal 1,260 days (3½ year period) right before Jesus' Second Coming. However, he also taught that the Millennium was not a literal thousand years, but the period of time between the cross and the antichrist (Amillennialism).[25] And in England after the Reformation, "William Tyndale (1480–1536), John Bradford (Chaplain to Edward the VI), Nicholas Ridley (Bishop of London), Hugh Latimer, and Thomas Cranmer (English Archbishop, 1489–1556) all died for their Reformed faith, which included premillennialism." During the reign of Queen Elizabeth (1558–1603), Protestantism took hold in England and premillennial thought could be found in the liturgies and prayers of that time. These English Puritans became the founding fathers of the "Independents, Presbyterians and Baptists of Great Britain."[26] And in 1643, the Westminster Assembly was convened to establish the doctrines of the Church of England. Many of the 151 attendees were expressed Premillennialists. The results of the Assembly were various statements of the premillennial view of the Lord's Return in the *Shorter Catechism, Larger Catechism*, and the *Directory of Public Worship*.[27] Yet, it was primarily the Anabaptists and the Puritans who carried on the premillennial view.

The Puritan millennial fervor was transferred to America upon their arrival with a Columbus-like vision of setting up the New

Jerusalem or "City on a Hill" in the New World.[28] Gradually, the focus shifted from the same as their English counterparts in Europe to the vision of bringing Christ's kingdom in their new holy Christian commonwealth. Among these American Puritans, who were seen as a mix of pre- and post-millennialists, there remained very strong voices in Increase (1639–1723) and Cotton (1663–1728) Mather for standard Premillennialism. In fact, Cotton Mather "inaugurated an era of apocalyptic expectation in America that did not lose its force until after the American Revolution."[29]

The Puritans gradually gave way to Postmillennialism by the mid-eighteenth century, in most part due to the preaching of Jonathan Edwards in America[30] and the influences of John Locke and Salisbury Rector Daniel Whitby in England.[31] Yet in 1791, a Jesuit named Manuel de Lacunza (who was living in Imola, Italy) published *La Venida die Mesias en Gloria y Magestad* (*The Coming of Messiah in Glory and Majesty*) in Spanish under the pseudonym Juan Josafat Ben Ezra—outlining the Rapture of the Church, the appearance of the antichrist, the premillennial Second Advent of Christ, and then, the Millennial Reign of Christ on earth. This was a huge step for a member of the Roman Catholic Church, especially a Jesuit. But it actually did more to unite portions of the Catholic and Protestant Churches than anything else in nearly three hundred years. All of this and the occurrence of the French Revolution (1790s) lead up to the rebirth of Premillennialism in both England and America in the nineteenth and twentieth centuries.[32] It was at this point, that Postmillennialism and Amillennialism began to fade as the Protestant Church's dominant belief.

This renewed Premillennialism was fueled in England by Edward Irving, an Anglican Pastor, who moved from Scotland to London to take a parish in 1822. By 1826, Irving had translated Lacunza's *The Coming of Messiah in Glory and*

Majesty into English, and along with James Hatley Frere (a Scottish Presbyterian) and Lewis Way (who founded the London Society for Promoting Christianity Among Jews, to help Jews to return to Palestine and rebuild their homeland) established the "Society for the Investigation of Prophecy" and began preaching on premillennial eschatology.[33] About the same time, John Nelson (J. N.) Darby and Benjamin Wills Newton began to turn away from the secularness and laxness of the Church of England. Consequently, they formed an independent group called the Plymouth Brethren, with a focus on apostolic Christianity and Premillennialism. Ultimately, Darby and Newton split into the two different forms of Premillennialism: <u>Historicists</u>, who believed that most of the events described by Daniel and John in Revelation were being fulfilled in European history; and <u>Futurists</u>, who believed none of these events had occurred yet and would occur at the end of the dispensation of the Church, just prior to the Second Advent (also called Dispensationalists).[34]

While in America about the same time period, William Miller (a self-educated farmer from upstate New York and converted in 1816 by the Baptists) had developed his own version of Historicist Premillennialism from his personal study of Bible prophecy. The main differences between his and the British form were the following beliefs: the Jews were not to be restored to Palestine, no non-believers would survive the Second Coming, and the firm conviction of a specific date for the Second Coming around 1843.[35] Thus, Miller was "the most famous millenarian in American History,"[36] and, "Darby systemized dispensationalism and spread its major principles throughout the English-speaking world."[37] From this point in the nineteenth century, the Premillennial Dispensational Movement exploded both in England and the United States and gave rise to more theologians (mostly Plymouth Brethren, Baptists, and Presbyterians).[38]

After the turn of the twentieth century, two new leaders took over the Darby dispensationalist mantle and continued to spread its views: Arno C. Gaebelein, a German immigrant and Methodist minister who established a monthly paper in New York City, *Our Hope*, with a two-fold purpose of proclaiming the imminent Second Coming and the Zionist Awakening among the Jews; and Cyrus I. (C. I.) Scofield, who was raised in Tennessee, fought in the Civil War under Lee, converted in St. Louis in 1879, and became Pastor of First Congregational Church in Dallas, and then, the Moody Church in Northfield, Massachusetts. Scofield came up with the idea for a dispensational chain-reference Bible while strolling on the Massachusetts beach in 1901. He started work on it in 1902 and produced the first draft in 1908.[39] During the period 1901–1914, Gaebelein reinvigorated the movement by espousing pretribulational Darbyism and fighting growing liberalism in the Church.[40]

About this same time came the birth of *The Fundamentals*, a paper devoted to describing the movement that married conservatives and millenarians in the fight against Modernism, Progressivism, and Liberalism. This paper was the brainchild of Lyman Stewart, a shy, retiring businessman, with the help of Rev. A. C. Dixon. It ran from 1910–1915. At the outset, they established "Seven Articles of Doctrine" that closely aligned with Darbyism. The intent was to pick up the movement where the Millenarians had left off.[41] All this activity carried the Millenarian Movement to the brink of WWI, which in and of itself renewed the public interest in prophecy (especially after the British captured Jerusalem in May, 1918).

Scofield died in 1921, and Gaebelein continued with *Our Hope* and became a prolific writer, but stopped speaking at conferences. Finally in 1919, at the first meeting of the World's Conference on Christian Fundamentals, the Millenarians officially changed their name to Fundamentalists and continued to fight battles with the Liberals and Modernists (one of the biggest being against the "theory of evolution" in the 1920s).[42] The Fundamentalists became absorbed primarily into the Presbyterian and Baptist denominations. However, their Premillennialism began to spread to the early twentieth-century American revival-based Pentecostal and Holiness denominations, and ultimately to the Pentecostals, Evangelicals, and Charismatics of the 1950s, 60s, and 70s.[43]

Based upon a Premillennial-Futuristic view, and since the concept of the Millennium is closely related to the Old Testament concept of the Kingdom of Heaven/God and related covenants (Abrahamic, Mosaic, Davidic, and New) on earth through the Messianic Kingdom, let us now explore those particular Old Testament prophecies. Many of these prophecies are located in the same passages of scripture as noted in certain *Parousia* prophecies addressed in the previous chapter.[44] Also, there are those scripture verses that deal only with the restoration of Israel, Jerusalem, and the Temple.[45]

Finally, there are the prophetic scriptures that specifically deal with the Millennial or Messianic Kingdom from a literal and physical perspective. It has its center or capital in Jerusalem (Obad 15–21), from which the world will be governed (Isa 2:3; 24:23). The kingdom is ruled by a real king (both human—Isa 11:1–5; 33:14–17; Dan 7:13–14—and divine—Ps 2:6–7; Isa 9:6; 40:9–10), sitting on a real throne (Isa 33:17), and who fulfills the Davidic Covenant (2 Sam 7:8–16; Ps 89:3–4, 34–37; Jer 33:15–22) with a revived Davidic Kingdom (Amos 9:11; Acts 16–18). And, all the nations and kingdoms of the earth will be destroyed at the coming of that king—the King of Kings (Dan 2:31–45).[46]

Prophecies also specifically address this literal kingdom's "manifestation," or timing and process of events in human history—worldwide judgments via the sun, moon, stars, earthquakes, floods, fire, famine, and pestilence (Isa 24; Joel 2:30–31; 3:9–15), followed by the coming of the divine kingdom (Isa 40:5; Ezek 20:33–38; Dan 2:34, 44; Matt 25:31–46).[47] The kingdom's "form of government" will be "monarchical," but also a theocracy, with God ruling and reigning with "a rod of iron" and "righteousness." Yet still, He will "gather the lambs in His arms, carry them in His bosom, and gently lead those that are with young" (Ps 2:6–9, 12; Isa 9:6–7; 11:4; 32:1; 33:17–24; 40:11; Dan 7:14; Zech 14:9).[48] The kingdom will have an "external organization," with delegated governance to three groups of resurrected saints: the Old Testament saints (Ezek 37:24–25; Dan 7:18, 22, and 27); the Church (1 Cor 6:2; Rev 3:21; 20:6); and the tribulation martyrs (Rev 20:4), given charge over the redeemed Jews and Gentiles entering the Millennium.[49] And the kingdom's "essential nature" will be "spiritual in nature" and "ethical" in "conduct," restoring "perfect social relations" and thus causing "physical   transformation…political   changes…religious purification".[50]

From these prophetic Old Testament scriptures, it may be concluded that the concept of the Millennial Kingdom was established by *Yahweh* in the Old Testament as the fulfillment of His original desire to dwell among His creation on earth (as outlined in Gen 2–3 in the Garden of Eden), using all the related concepts addressed above (the Messianic First Advent of Jesus, the Kingdom of Heaven/God, the Messianic Second Advent/*Parousia* of Jesus, the restoration of Israel, and the Millennial Kingdom) to convey the thought. This is confirmed by Jesus and His ministry and the continuation of that ministry by the Apostles in New Testament times. With this basic understanding of the Millennium, and assuming a Premillennial Futurist view of it, we can now go on to the next part of the *Parousia* to discuss—the Day of the Lord (*Yahweh*).

7.

What Is the Day of the Lord (*Yahweh*), the Tribulation?

The Day of the LORD (*Yahweh*) is an Old Testament term that becomes contextualized by the eschatological writings in the New Testament. The term "Day of the LORD (*Yahweh*)" is mentioned by the following Old Testament prophets in their respective texts: Isaiah 2:6–21; 13:6–13; Jeremiah 30:7 (called "Jacob's trouble," or distress);[1] Ezekiel 30:2–3; Joel 1:15; 2:1–2, 10–11, 30–31; 3:14–16; Amos 5:18–20; Obadiah 15; Zephaniah 1:14–2:3; Zechariah 14:1–4, and Malachi 4:1–5. In all these Old Testament passages, the Day of LORD is characterized as a time of thick darkness, gloominess, judgment, trouble, distress, and terror. During the Day of the LORD, these scriptures indicate that God will pour out His "wrath," destruction, punishment, vengeance, and fire upon the earth for its evil, sin, and iniquity at some time in the future.[2] Therefore in general terms, the "Day of the LORD" is when the "wrath of God" will be poured out upon the earth because of sin(s).

The clear New Testament references to the Day of the Lord (Acts 2:19–20 [restatement of Joel 2:30–31 in Peter's sermon on the Day of Pentecost]; 1 Thess 5:2–4; 2 Thess 2:1–5; and 2 Pet 3:5–10) place it within the context of Daniel's "seventieth week," addressed by Daniel 9:24–27 and 12:1–2. This concept of "seventy weeks of years" (or 490 years) is specifically addressed in Daniel 9:24–27: describing 69 of the 70 weeks of years (or 483 out of 490 years)—in verses 25–26—which were fulfilled from the decree to restore and rebuild Jerusalem (given by King Artaxerxes in 445 BC—Neh 2:1–8) to Jesus the Messiah's death and resurrection in approximately AD 31–35 (see chapter 3 for more specific detail). The remaining "seventieth week" (or seven years) is also commonly referred to as the Seven-year Tribulation Period addressed in Daniel 9:27; 12:1–2, Matthew 24:15–31, Mark 13:14–27, Luke 21:24b–28, and Revelation 6–8. This 7-year period is also commonly broken into two 3½-year periods (per Dan 9:27: "but in the middle of the week"), with the latter 3½ year period also being known as the "Great Tribulation" (Matt 24:21; Rev 7:14). Thus, the Day of the LORD or the Tribulation is an *unprecedented seven-year period of God's wrath (Dan 12:1)* poured out on humanity for the cumulative sin on the earth for approximately six thousand years of human history.[3] On a related note and per the eternal covenant God made with Noah and all humanity after him in Genesis 9:8–17, God promised never again to destroy all humanity, the animals, and the earth with a flood. But as Peter adds in 2 Peter 3:5–10: even though the earth will not be destroyed by another flood during the Day of the Lord, the heavens and the earth "will be destroyed with intense heat…and…burned up."

Many things happen during the Seven-year Tribulation—which are primarily contained in Revelation 6–19—and will be more specifically addressed below. But before the Seven-year Tribulation begins, Paul states in 1 Thessalonians 1:10 and 5:1–10 that God will *deliver* Christians from this wrath to come, and "did not appoint" them for this "wrath" associated with the Day of the Lord, but *salvation* through Jesus Christ (the complete salvation addressed by the Perfect/Complete Gospel). Therefore according to this understanding, Christians (the Body of Christ/the Church) will not be on the earth during the Tribulation, when God pours out His wrath. This is confirmed by the Church being removed as the "what" or "he…restrains"

(2 Thess 2:6–7) the "man of lawlessness…the son of destruction" (2 Thess 2:3b–12) _before the Day of the Lord (2 Thess 2:2)._[4] _This "man of lawlessness/son of destruction" will be further discussed below. And, the Church being removed as the restrainer of the man of lawlessness/son of destruction (also termed the "Rapture of the Church") will be specifically addressed in the next chapter (chap. 8). Thus, this removal of the Church from the earth represents the end of the Church Age and the beginning of the Day of the Lord or the Seven-year Tribulation Period._[5]

With the void left on the earth by this departure of the Church, the man of lawlessness/son of destruction will take over. He is also known as: the "little horn," which arose from the ten horns on the fourth beast, and who destroyed three of the first ten horns, in Daniel 7:7–8, 19–26; the "king of the north" in Daniel 11:40–45; the rider on "a white horse" with a "bow" and a "crown" in Revelation 6:1–2; "the beast coming out of the sea" in Revelation 13:1–10 (Rev 14:9, 11; 15:2; 16:2; 17:3, 13; 19:20; and 20:10); or the Antichrist mentioned in 1 John 2:18; 4:3; and 2 John 7. Although the Antichrist (literally, "against, or in opposition to," Christ)[6] may not be the best name for this End-time, satanic leader of the world against Jesus and the Kingdom of God, it is the most well-known and will be used from here on.

So after the Church is removed from the earth, the Antichrist is revealed at the beginning of the Seven-year Tribulation Period and makes a covenant "with the many" for seven years (Dan 9:27; Rev 6:1–2). He arises out of a Ten-Nation Confederacy and subdues three of the ten nations (Dan 2:41–44; 7:7–8, 20–24; Rev 13:1–3a). And then, he steps in as the satanic leader, ruler, and king of the world for the entire Tribulation Period (Dan 7:25; 11:40–45a; 2 Thess 2:3b–4, 8–9; Rev 3b–10), in direct opposition to the true Kings of Kings—Jesus Christ.

Additionally, the Antichrist is aided by the "False Prophet" (the second beast, "coming up out of the earth" in Rev 13:11–18) for the last 3½ years of the Tribulation, until they are both destroyed at the end of the Tribulation by Jesus' Second Coming (Dan 2:45; 7:26–27; 11:45b; 2 Thess 2:8b; Rev 19:17–21). Another name for the Antichrist, False Prophet, and Satan, or the "dragon" of Revelation 12:3–9 (who empowers them both) is the "unholy trinity" or "trinity of hell" (Rev 16:13).[7]

Over Church History, there have been many descriptions or names of whom the Antichrist was or will be (e.g., a Jew from the Tribe of Dan, one of the Caesars, one of the political leaders of Europe, Russia, or the United States, the Pope, or whoever's name adds up to 666—"the number of the beast"—Rev 13:18). And yet, he will more than likely be an Islamic Antichrist, probably from the region in or around Syria, for the following reasons. Since he will rise out of and lead the Ten-Nation Confederacy of Daniel 2:41–44; 7:7–8, 20–24, and Revelation 13:1–3a, we need to determine which ten nations those are. Most theologians believe that they will come from the region of the old Roman Empire (the legs of Iron of Nebuchadnezzar's statue of Dan 2:33, 40 and the fourth beast of Dan 7:7, 19, 23): as the ten toes of partly of iron and partly of clay of Nebuchadnezzar's statue (Dan 2:41–44) and the ten horns on the fourth beast of Daniel 7:7, 24. And as such, many of those theologians believe that the formation of the Common Market, European Economic Community (EEC), or the European Union (EU) in the late 1950s fulfilled those prophecies.[8] Over time, the membership did work its way up to ten nations; but then, it superseded that number. So as of today, the number of member nations in the EU is twenty-eight.

However in the mid-1980s, two theologians proposed the Ten-nation Confederacy to be an Arab/Islamic Confederation based on Psalm 83. In that psalm, ten nations or people groups

(Edomites, Ishmaelites, Moabites, Hagrites, Gebalites, Ammonites, Amalekites, and people of Philistia and Tyre, and Assyria) collectively say, *"Come, and let us wipe them out as a nation, that the name of Israel be remembered no more* [emphasis added]. For they have conspired together with one mind; Against You they make a covenant" (Ps 83:4–8). And the psalmist adds in verse 13, "O my God, *make them like the whirling dust, like chaff before the wind* [emphasis added]." This is the exact same language that is used in Daniel 2:34–35, 45 to speak of the destruction of the Ten-nation Confederacy by the "rock cut not by human hands" (Messiah Jesus) in the future! These ten Old Testament nations mentioned in Psalm 83 basically correspond to part of or all of the following modern Arab/Islamic nations: Jordan, Saudi Arabia, Kuwait, Iraq, Egypt, Lebanon, the Palestinians (PLO), Syria, Iran, and Turkey.[9] Thus, it appears that the Antichrist will come from one of these ten Islamic nations. And more than likely, he will most probably come from Syria (as his predecessor, Antiochus IV [Epiphanes], 175–164 BC, did to fulfill the prophecies in Dan 8:9–14, 23–26 and 11:21–39).

Several more recent books talk about this "Islamic Antichrist" more specifically. They correlate the "Twelfth Imam" or "the Mahdi" ("the Guided One") of Islam to be the Antichrist, to arise and fulfill these prophecies in Daniel and Revelation. In summary, the following are the characteristics or signs from Islamic eschatological writings about the Mahdi that relate to the prophecies about the Antichrist. He will: "be an unparalleled spiritual, political, and military world leader"; arise "after a period of great turmoil and suffering upon the earth"; establish worldwide justice, righteousness, and "eradicate tyranny and oppression"; be the "leader of Muslims worldwide"; "lead a world revolution and establish a new world order"; "lead military action against all those who oppose him"; "invade many countries"; "make a seven-year peace treaty with a Jew of priestly lineage"; "conquer Israel for Islam and lead the 'faithful Muslims' in a final slaughter/battle against the Jews"; "rule for seven years"; "appear riding a white horse"; "rediscover the Ark of the Covenant from the Sea of Galilee, which he will bring to Jerusalem"; "have supernatural power from Allah over the wind and the rain and crops"; and "be loved by all the people of the earth."[10] Another book correlates this to a "Seven-Phase Manifesto of the Antichrist" as follows: "Phase 1: Take Control of Israel" (per Dan 11:45); "Phase 2: Take Control of Jerusalem" (per Luke 21:24); "Phase 3: Convert the World to His Own Religion" (per Rev 13:4); "Phase 4: Destroy all Opposition to His Control" (per Dan 11:44 and Rev 20:4); "Phase 5: Control all Buying and Selling" (per Rev 13:16–17); "Phase 6: Control the Temple Mount in Jerusalem" (per Rev 11:1–2); and "Phase 7: Be Worshipped as God" (per 2 Thess 2:4 and Rev 13:4).[11] From all this information, one can see that this Islamic Antichrist from the region in or around Syria pretty much matches the Antichrist described in the Bible. Next, we will begin to address other issues and events that happen during the Tribulation.

The removal of the Church (Body of Christ) from the earth before the Tribulation begins will leave behind unbelieving Jews (Nation of Israel), who have not accepted Jesus as Messiah, and unbelieving Gentiles (Gentile nations). The Gentile nations will then be primarily grouped as follows. There will be a Ten-Nation Arab Confederacy under control of the Antichrist (Ps 83; Dan 2:44; 7:7b–8, 24; Rev 13:1–3; 17:12–14)—as outlined above.[12] There will be a Northern Confederacy, which is primarily described by Ezekiel 38:2–6, and made up of "Gog of the land of Magog, the prince of Rosh, Meshech and Tubal…Persia, Ethiopia, and Put…Gomer…Beth-togarmah from the remote parts of the north." These Old Testament nations correspond to the parts of or all of the following modern countries: southern Russia, north and northeast of the Black Sea and east of the Aral Sea; Turkey; Iran; Ethiopia/Sudan; Libya; and Armenia (note that there is some overlap with the Ten-Nation Confederacy). This Northern Confederacy will oppose both Antichrist's Ten-Nation Confederacy and attack Israel.[13] Next, there will be the "kings from the East," or the Asiatic Confederacy of Revelation 16:12, who join with the other armies of the earth to come against Israel in the Battle of Armageddon (Rev 16:16; 19:17–21).[14] And finally, there will be the "King of the South," the N. African Confederacy, or Egypt, Libya, and Sudan/Ethiopia in Daniel 11:40–43, who will join with Antichrist and the Ten-Nation Confederacy to come against Israel.[15]

As mentioned above, the 7 years of the Tribulation are broken into two 3½ year periods per Daniel 9:27, with the latter 3½ year period being known as the Great Tribulation (or Jacob's trouble). This seven-year period may be broken down further by Revelation 6–19 as follows: the first 3½ years of the Tribulation (Rev 5–7; 8:1–5; 13:1–2); Mid-Tribulation (Dan 9:24; Rev 7:9–17; 11:1–4; 12:13–17; 13:2–18; 14:1–7; 17:16–18; and 2 Thess 2:3–4); and the last 3½ years, or Great Tribulation (Rev 8:6–10; 11:5–19; 14:8–16).[16] Next, each period will be specifically addressed.

During the first 3½ years of the Tribulation, the "seven seals" are broken on "the scroll" with "writing on the inside and outside of the scroll" given to Jesus ("the Lion from the tribe of Judah, the Root of David...a Lamb standing, as if slain, having seven horns and seven eyes, which are the seven Spirits of God") by God the Father in heaven (Rev 5). This represents the following events taking place on earth, described seal-by-seal. After the "first seal" is broken, the Antichrist is revealed as a "rider on a white horse," carrying "a bow, and a crown was placed on his head. He rode out to win many battles and gain the victory" (Rev 6:1–2). He also will make a seven-year covenant with Israel (Dan 9:27). Next, the "second through fourth seals" are broken, and the other three of the "Four Horsemen of the Apocalypse," riding red, black, and pale green horses respectively, *destroy one-fourth of the earth's population* at that time by war, famine, pestilence, and death (Rev 6:3–8)! Then, the "fifth seal" is broken, and many of the Tribulation Saints are identified as being martyred for their faith (Rev 6:9–11). As the "sixth seal" is broken, nature's upheaval is identified by a "great earthquake…sun became as dark as black cloth…moon became as red as blood" and "the stars of the sky fell to earth…" (Rev 6:12–17). But, the complete upheaval of the earth is postponed until the end of the Tribulation.[17]

And before the breaking of the "seventh seal," the vision given to John pans back to heaven, and focuses on the Nation of Israel left behind after the Church was removed before the Tribulation began. This vision also applies to the entire first 3½ years, and shows God's plan in lieu of the Church witnessing about Jesus being the Messiah. In Revelation 7:1–8, 144,000 Jewish "servants" or witnesses (12,000 from each of the 12 tribes of Israel—two tribes being named for Joseph [Joseph and Manasseh] and leaving out the tribe of Dan) are released to act as witnesses on the earth, primarily, if not exclusively, to the Nation of Israel. Then at the end of the first 3½ years, there appears "a vast crowd, too great to count, from every nation and tribe and people and language, standing before the throne and" before Jesus in heaven (Rev 7:9–17). This probably represents the "rapture" of Tribulation Saints (both Jews and Gentiles) who have not already been martyred and are converts from the 144,000's ministry before the beginning of the last 3½ years or Great Tribulation.[18]

Then in Revelation 8:1–5, the "seventh seal" is broken, and "there was silence throughout heaven for about half an hour." This signifies the beginning of the Mid-Tribulation events that occur, or start, before the beginning of the Great Tribulation (last 3½ years). These Mid-Tribulation events are as follows:

1) Antichrist breaks the covenant with Israel, sets up the "Abomination of Desolation" (Dan 9:27; cf. Matt 24:15), destroys the world religious "harlot" (one-world religion of Rev 17:16–18), and declares himself to be God in the Temple (2 Thess 2:3–4);

2) the False Prophet starts the "mark of the Beast" (Rev 13:16–18) and idol worship (Rev 13:14–15);

3) Antichrist then attacks Israel, but God hides them away for 3½ years, and he turns his attention to the remaining people alive in the Great Tribulation (Rev 12:13–17);

4) the Two Witnesses begin their ministry (Rev 11:1–4); and

5) the angelic ministry of the Gospel begins (Rev 14:6–12).[19]

Finally, after the Mid-Tribulation events and after the "silence in heaven for half an hour," the Great Tribulation begins with "seven angels given seven trumpets to blow" (Rev 8:2–6). Next, the first four angels blow their trumpets and the following plagues are released: "First Trumpet"—hail and fire, mingled with blood, and one-third of the trees and all green grass is burned up; "Second Trumpet"—a great mountain of fire is thrown into the sea, and one-third of the sea becomes blood, one-third of the sea-creatures die, and one-third of the ships are destroyed; "Third Trumpet"—a great star named Wormwood falls from the sky on one-third of the rivers and springs of water, and one-third of the fresh water becomes bitter *and many people died from the bitter water*; "Fourth Trumpet"—one-third of the sun, moon, and stars are struck, and so, one-third of all the light is darkened (Rev 8:7–12). Then, preparation is made for the final three trumpets to sound, unleashing the final three "woes" or terrors (Rev 8:13).[20]

When the "Fifth Trumpet" (or "First Woe") is sounded, a plague of demon-controlled locusts that sting like scorpions begins and lasts for five months. These "locusts" will not hurt the grass or plants, but only "people who did not have of the seal of God on their foreheads" (Rev 9:1–4). This indicates that the 144,000 (who were sealed on their foreheads in Rev 7:3–4) are still witnessing, and probably are with the Nation of Israel "fled into the wilderness," where God had prepared a place to give her care for 3½ years (Rev 12:6, 13–16). However, the locusts will torture, but not kill, the others on the earth for the five months (Rev 9:1–12). Yet it appears that after the "Fifth Trumpet" and before the "Sixth Trumpet," the 144,000 will be raptured to heaven with Jesus per Revelation 14:1–5.[21]

Then after the Sixth Trumpet (or Second Woe) is sounded, four demons, "who are bound at the great Euphrates River," are released to lead "an army of 200 million mounted troops" to *kill one-third of the people left on the earth* (Rev 9:13–19). Please note: *With the one-fourth of the earth's population destroyed by the "Second through Fourth Seals," plus the many others by the "Third Trumpet," added to this one-third of the remaining population, during the "Sixth Trumpet," **approximately 60% of the earth's population during the Tribulation will have died!*** But even after all of that, the people who remain will still refuse to repent of their idol-worship, murders, witchcraft, immorality, and thefts (Rev 9:20–21).[22]

After the Sixth Trumpet, the Two Witnesses' ministry is described during the last 3½ years, ending in their deaths and leading up to the blowing of the "Seventh Trumpet"/"Third Woe" (Rev 11:4–14). A short discussion on the Two Witnesses is warranted here. They are also referred to as "prophets" and "the two olive trees and the two lampstands that stand before the Lord" (Rev 11:4; see also Zech 4:11–14). There has been much speculation regarding their identities. But based on everything that they do during the Great Tribulation (fire consuming their enemies, power to stop the rain, power to turn oceans and rivers to blood, and send any plague upon the earth), their deaths, bodies lying in Jerusalem for 3½ days, and resurrections and raptures (Rev 11:5–12), I believe that the two most likely candidates are Enoch and Elijah (both who did not die and were raptured to heaven—see Gen 5:24; Heb 11:5; 2 Kgs 2:11). In any case, after the Two Witnesses are raptured there is a "great earthquake" and "*seven thousand people died*" (Rev 11:13). This is all in preparation for the "Seventh Trumpet" ("Third Woe").[23]

Then in Revelation 11:15, the "Seventh Trumpet" is blown, beginning the final thirty days (see Dan 12:11–12) and end of the Great Tribulation. After the blowing of the seventh and final trumpet, Revelation 15 and 16 describe the final "seven bowls of seven plagues" to be poured out on the earth (malignant sores; entire sea turned to blood and everything in it dies; all the fresh water turns to blood; the sun scorches the entire earth with fire; followed by the kingdom of the Antichrist being turned to darkness; the Euphrates River dries up, driving the armies and kings from the east to march to battle, along with all the other kings of the earth, to the Battle of Armageddon [which is previewed in Rev 14:14–20, with the blood flowing for about 180 miles and 4 feet high]; and thunder, lightning, the greatest earthquake of all time, and giant [75 lb.] hailstones).[24] This all culminates with all the kings mentioned above and their armies being gathered together at the Battle of Armageddon and being destroyed by Jesus ("the Word of God" and "King of kings and Lord of lords") in Revelation 6:16–21 and 19:11–21. However as a reminder: despite all the plagues, war, destruction, and death during the Tribulation, the Holy Spirit will still be present on the earth to dispense God's grace, mercy, Word, and salvation through the 144,000 Jewish Witnesses of Revelation 7:1–8; 14:1–5; the Two Witnesses of Revelation 11; the angelic ministry of Revelation 14:6–20; and all those who become believers and also witness during the Tribulation.[25]

Following the Battle of Armageddon and the Second Coming of Jesus of Revelation 19:11–21, Satan is bound in "the bottomless pit" for one thousand years in Revelation 20:1–3 (see chap. 6 for a discussion on the Millennium). And, this ends the Tribulation Period (or the Day of the Lord). It is generally understood by theologians that at this point in time, Jesus will fulfill the prophecy in Zechariah 14:3–5 by standing on the Mount of Olives, which will split apart. Then, Jesus will dispense the various judgments and resurrections reserved for that time (see chap. 9). But before we can address that, the next chapter will back up and address the Church's departure before the Tribulation Period, also known as the "Rapture of the Church."

8.

What Is the Rapture of the Church?

All those who hold the premillennial-futurist view of eschatology believe that the Rapture of the Church (which includes the Church/universal Body of Christ from the entire Church Age—approximately two thousand years) will occur as part of the *Parousia* (all the events surrounding the Second Coming of Jesus—defined in chapter 5), and that the primary Rapture references in the Bible were written by Paul in 1 Thessalonians 4:13–18 and 1 Corinthians 15:51–57. As discussed in the previous chapter (7), on the Day of the Lord/ Tribulation, the Rapture of the Church will more than likely take place before the Tribulation per 1 Thessalonians 1:10 and 5:1–10. In these passages, Paul states that God will "deliver" Christians from, and "did not appoint" them, for this "wrath" associated with the Day of the Lord, but salvation through Jesus Christ (the complete salvation addressed by the Perfect/ Complete Gospel). And according to this understanding, Christians (the Body of Christ/the Church) will not be on the earth during the Tribulation, when God pours out His wrath. This is confirmed by the understanding that the Church will "be removed" as the "what" or "he...restrains" (2 Thess 2:6–7) the "man of lawlessness...the son of destruction" (2 Thess 2:3b–12) *before the Day of the Lord (2 Thess 2:2).*[1] *Again, please see the previous chapter for this discussion.*

Next, please note the following treatment of the word "rapture" taken from my master's thesis on the subject. The word rapture does not appear in the text of the Bible. However, it comes from the Latin words *rapere*, meaning "rapid"[2] and *rapiemur*, meaning, "We shall be caught up."[3] These words were taken from the Greek verb *harpazo* (which is in the Greek New Testament), meaning, "to seize upon, spoil, snatch away or take to oneself," especially used of rapture (Acts 8:39; 2 Cor 12:2, 4; 1 Thess 4:17; and Rev 12:5). The word *harpazo* is literally translated, "caught up" or "caught away" the five times (out of thirteen) it appears in the New Testament relating to rapture. The other eight times it is translated, "to forcibly seize upon, snatch away, take to oneself or use force on someone."[4]

In Acts 8:39, the Holy Spirit "caught away" Philip after he ministered to the Ethiopian eunuch, and placed him in Azotus (some 20–30 miles away). In 2 Corinthians 12:2–4, Paul twice describes his experience of being "caught up" to the Third Heaven. In Revelation 12:5, "a son, male child" (usually interpreted to mean Jesus) of "a woman clothed with the sun, and the moon under her feet, and on her head a crown of twelve stars" (Rev 12:1, and usually interpreted to mean the Nation of Israel) was "caught up to God and His throne" (speaking of Jesus' ascension or rapture in Acts 1:9–11). And in 1 Thessalonians 4:17, the primary text for the Rapture of the Church, Paul explains, "we who are alive and remain shall be *caught up* [emphasis added] together with them in the clouds, to meet the Lord in the air, and thus we shall always be with the Lord." The phrase "together with them" in this verse refers to the "dead in Christ," who were resurrected immediately preceding the Rapture of the Church.[5]

As mentioned above, the other primary Rapture passage is 1 Corinthians 15:51–55: "Behold, I tell you a mystery; we shall not all sleep [in death], but we shall all be *changed*, in a moment in the twinkling of an eye, at the last trumpet; for the trumpet will sound and the dead will be raised imperishable, and we shall be *changed* [emphasis added]." While the concept of rapture is represented by the Greek word *harpazo* in 1 Thessalonians 4:17, it is represented by the Greek word *allasso* ("to change the form or nature of a thing")[6] in 1 Corinthians 15:51–52, within the context of the resurrection of the Church. The word *allasso* is related to two other Greek verbs that are tied to the rapture concept. The first is *metatithemi*, meaning "to transpose, put in another place and hence to transfer, translate"—used in both Genesis 5:24 (in the Septuagint [LXX], the Greek translation of the Old Testament) and Hebrews 11:5 to describe the translation of Enoch to heaven.[7] And the second is *metamorphoo*, meaning "to transform, transfigure, or change one's form"—used to describe Jesus' appearance on the Mount of Transfiguration (Matt 17:1–9; Mark 9:2–9; Luke 9:28–36), and "which suggests what the bodies of the righteous may be as a result of the resurrection of our bodies (1 Cor 15:51f)."[8] As can be seen by all these words relating to rapture, the focus for this event occurs in conjunction with the "resurrection of the body" (both individually and corporately as the Body of Christ) during the *Parousia*.

The relationship between the rapture and the resurrection of the Church poses a question about the distinction between the two, since they appear to happen almost simultaneously in the scripture passages mentioned above. The following quote from the master's thesis explicitly deals with the comparison between the terms "rapture" and "resurrection":

> Another term to be defined and placed in juxtaposition to rapture is resurrection (mostly the verb, *egeiro*, meaning "to rise, have risen" and the noun, *anastasis*, meaning "a standing up, a resurrection or recovery").[9] Resurrection speaks about the same type of raising or taking up as *harpazo*, but in reference to the dead or "sleeping" versus the living. In other words, [resurrection is] *raising the dead bodily back to life in a new incorruptible, immortal body compared to transporting or translating the living bodily to heaven.* Jesus is the first example of this resurrection.

102 Soon and Very Soon

Then, there will be those who are His (asleep/dead in Christ) at His "coming," [the *Parousia*] immediately preceding the Rapture (1 Cor 15:20–23, 50–52 and 1 Thess 4:16–17). Rapture and resurrection are very closely related, yet still completely separate and distinct concepts. *Therefore, Jesus' resurrection and ascension (rapture) at the beginning of the Church Age act as the type, model, or precedent for the resurrection and Rapture of His Body (the Church) at the end of the Church Age.*[10]

However, the question remains as to *when* during the *Parousia* will the Rapture of the Church occur? And more specifically, when will that "blessed hope" (Titus 2:13) occur in relation to the Seven-year Tribulation and the revealing of the Antichrist? As mentioned previously in chapter 6 on the Millennium, the answer to these questions may be divided into three different categories: pretribulational, midtribulational, and posttribulational. The proponents of all three positions agree that the Church (Body of Christ) will not be the target of God's wrath, to be poured out during the Tribulation or Day of the Lord (addressed in chapter 7). However, each position believes that the Rapture of the Church will occur at a different time in relation to the Seven-year Tribulation Period. Each of the positions will now be addressed in detail.

The pretribulational position believes the Rapture will occur prior to the revealing of the Antichrist and the subsequent start of the Tribulation Period. This event will be separate and distinct from the Second Coming of Jesus Christ to judge the earth (at the end of the Tribulation Period), as addressed in Matthew 24, Mark 13, Luke 21, and Revelation 19. This position is based on a literal-grammatical reading of the two primary Rapture passages (1 Thess 4:13–18 and 1 Cor 15:51–57), and is supported by the related passages addressed on the next page. This may best be seen by the following paraphrase of another author at the end of his nine-page exegetical study on 1 Thessalonians 4:15–17:

For this we say unto you by a revelation received from the Lord, that we that are alive, that are still surviving *when the parousia of the Lord begins*, shall in no way be ahead of them that are already dead. For the Lord Himself shall come down from heaven with a shouted command (to the dead in Christ)—in an archangel-like voice—and with God's last trumpet-call (to Israel to deal with them again as a nation): and the dead in Christ shall stand up (be resurrected) first; *then we that are alive, that are left, shall together with them be snatched away from the people on earth, rescued from the fiery judgments of the tribulation about to begin, and caught up in clouds, to meet the Lord at a glorious reception in the air: and so shall we ever be with the Lord* [emphasis added].[11]

Additionally, please note the following chart of the Rapture of the Church versus the Second Coming, depicting them as two separate and distinct events:

Rapture	Return
1. Christ comes *for* His own (John 14:3; 1 Thess. 14:17; 2 Thess. 2:1)	1. Christ comes *with* His own (1 Thess. 3:13; Jude 14; Rev. 19:14)
2. He comes in the *air* (1 Thess. 4:17)	2. He comes to the *earth* (Zech. 14:4; Acts 1:11)
3. He *claims* His bride (1 Thess. 4:16–17)	3. He comes *with* His bride (Rev. 19:6–14)
4. Removal of *believers* (1 Thess. 4:17)	4. Manifestation of *Christ* (Mal. 4:2)
5. *Only* His own see Him (1 Thess. 4:13–18)	5. *Every eye* shall see Him (Rev. 1:7)
6. *Tribulation* begins (2 Thess. 1:6–9)	6. Millennial *kingdom* begins (Rev. 20:1–7)
7. Saved are *delivered from wrath* (1 Thess. 1:10; 5:9)	7. Unsaved *experience the wrath of God* (Rev. 6:12–17)

Rapture	Return
8. No *signs* precede the Rapture (1 Thess. 5:1–3)	8. *Signs* precede the Second Coming (Luke 21:11, 15)[12]

Related scriptures that support a Pretribulation Rapture include the following: the foreshadowing of the Rapture in Psalm 7:6–7, Joel 2:32, and Zephaniah 2:1–3; the raptures of Enoch (Gen 5:21–24), Elijah (2 Kgs 2:10–12[11–12]), and Jesus Himself (Acts 1:9–11); and Luke 21:36; John 14:2–3; Romans 8:22–24 [23–24]; 1 Corinthians 15:20–26 [23]; Philippians 1:6; 3:20–21; 2 Thessalonians 1:7–2:17 [2:1, 3]; Titus 2:11–13; Hebrews 9:28; James 5:7–8; 2 Peter 3; 1 John 2:28; 3:2; Jude 20–23 [21, 23]; and Revelation 4:1; 12:5.[13] Additionally, the following Early Church Fathers and Writings also seem to support a Pretribulation Rapture, either directly (*The Shepherd of Hermas* 4.1–2; *The Didache* [*The Teaching of the Twelve Apostles*] 16.3–8, n.14, n.16, n.17; Irenaeus' *Against Heresies* 5.5.1; 29.1; 30.4; 31.2; 32.1; and Victorinus' *Commentary on the Apocalypse* 6.14; 15.1), or indirectly (Clement of Rome's, *First Epistle to the Corinthians* 23, 24, 34, 35; Polycarp's, *The Epistle to the Philippians* 2, 5, 6; *The Epistle of Barnabas* 4, 16, 21; Tertullian's, *A Treatise on the Soul* 50; Cyprian's, *Treatises of Cyprian* 7.21, 22, 23, 25; and Chrysostom's, *Homilies on Ephesians* 3, *Homilies on 1st Thessalonians* 8, and *Homilies on 2nd Thessalonians* 3).[14] After completing the research and writing of my master's thesis on the subject, it is my belief that the understanding of a Pretribulation Rapture of the Church was passed on by Jesus to the Apostles Paul, John, Peter, James, and Jude, then to the Early Church Fathers, who in turn, continued to spread it within the Early Church through their writings as a doctrine of the Early Church. This then formed the foundation for "the blessed hope" (Tit 2:13) of the Early Church and the Perfect/Complete Gospel of Both Comings of Jesus Christ.

There is, however, an alternate reading (interpretation) of the primary Rapture passage in 1 Thessalonians 4:17, which forms the basis for the posttribulational view. This may be best described by the treatment of the passage in *The Renaissance New Testament* (1998). In this view, the Rapture of the Church is placed in conjunction with the Resurrection of the Just, the Judgment Seat of Christ, the Battle of Armageddon, and the Second Coming of Christ, "in accordance with Revelation 11:15–18, 1 Corinthians 15:51, and Luke 14:14." Although this reading agrees that the Rapture will occur and the Body of Christ will meet the Lord in the air, it compares the meeting of the "bridegroom" and the "ten virgins" in Matthew 25:1, 6 and the meeting of Paul and the Roman Christians in Acts 28:15 to Jesus and the raptured saints in 1 Thessalonians 4:17. This belief claims that in all these cases, the ones that went to the meeting "retraced their steps and returned to whence they came." Therefore, since Jesus is coming to earth (at the Second Coming), and the Rapture occurs in conjunction with this eschatological event, the saints will return to earth with Jesus for judgment and to rule and reign with Him.[15] This is coupled with the posttribulational view that nowhere in the scriptural text is the Rapture specifically indicated as occurring before the Tribulation.[16] Additionally, several modern theologians believe that Paul wrote 1 Thessalonians 4–5 as an amplification of what Jesus taught the Disciples in the Olivet or Apocalyptic Discourse in Matthew 24, Mark 13, and Luke 21—in which, He included no mention of rapture separate from the Second Coming.[17] There are also the following Early Church Fathers' Writings which seem to support the posttribulation position: Hippolytus, *Treatise on Christ and Antichrist* 60, 61, 64, 66 and Cyril, *The Catechetical Lectures of S. Cyril* 15.19.[18]

However, there appear to be several problems with this posttribulational view. First, as mentioned above, the Rapture and the Second Coming have two completely different purposes. The Rapture is the specific *kairos* event in *chronos* time that will complete the Church Age (see chap. 7). And just as Jesus ascended into heaven in Acts 1:9–11 (after receiving His new resurrected body), the Body of Christ will do likewise, and remain in heaven during the Tribulation on earth to undergo the Judgment Seat of Christ (Rom 14:10–12; 1 Cor 3:11–14; and 2 Cor 5:10) and partake in the Marriage Supper of the Lamb (Rev 19:7–9). Both of these events will be discussed further in the next chapter (9). Conversely, the Second Coming of Christ (and the Day of the Lord/Tribulation that precedes it) will be for judgment on the earth because of sin and in fulfillment of the Old Testament Day of the Lord prophecies. The Second Coming will occur at the end of the Tribulation, in conjunction with the Battle of Armageddon (see chap. 7). At the Second Coming, the previously resurrected and raptured Body of Christ and the angels will return with Jesus (Rev 19:11–21).

Secondly, although God could, in His sovereignty, choose to have all these events occur simultaneously, it would appear to violate the historical-chronological-biblical, space-time continuum (which He established for humanity—see chap. 3) to do so. In this regard, God would be dealing with two different groups (saints and sinners), for two completely different reasons (completion of the Eschatological Gospel of Salvation and rewards versus judgment of sin and disposition of sinners) simultaneously! This posttribulation interpretation also conflicts with the Judgment Seat of Christ scriptures for the Church (listed above) and the Great White Throne scripture for Satan, the Beast, False Prophet, and sinners (Rev 20:10–15).

Lastly, by relating the bridegroom and ten virgins of Matthew 25 and Paul and the Roman Christians of Acts 28 to Jesus and the Rapture of the Church in 1 Thessalonians 4, this violates the first rule of hermeneutics (biblical interpretation): "a text without a context is a pretext." This view has taken two completely different contexts (Jesus personally teaching about the Kingdom of Heaven/God at the Second Coming in parable format, using a Jewish wedding analogy, and Luke historically recording the meeting of Paul and the Roman Christians on his way to imprisonment) and yoked them together with a third context of Paul teaching about the "mystery" or "revelation" of the Rapture of the Church (to take place in conjunction with the resurrection of the "dead in Christ" and in prophetic fulfillment of Jesus' resurrection and ascension and the Perfect/Complete Gospel of Salvation). However, it may be understandable to follow this logic, if one accepts the posttribulational argument that Paul *did not* receive a "new revelation" of the Rapture of the Church, but was just amplifying information about Jesus' Second Coming (as addressed above).[19] However, with all this taken into account, the alternate reading (advocating the posttribulational view) must be rejected as contextually, chronologically, and scripturally untenable.

The midtribulational position may be best described as follows: "According to mid-tribulation rapturists, the catching away of the church will occur three and one-half years into the Tribulation period, immediately prior to the Great Tribulation…that the wrath of God is to be associated only with the Great Tribulation and that this wrath will be triggered by the opening of the seventh trumpet judgment (Rev 11). Therefore, midtribulationists would view their position as teaching that the Rapture will exempt the church from God's judgment."[20] This position can be modified to move the Rapture farther into the Seven-year Tribulation Period (and is labelled the "Pre-Wrath Rapture")—occurring after the start of the Great Tribulation, but before the pouring out of God's wrath during "the Day of the Lord…about midway through the second three and one half years," using Matthew 24–25 in conjunction with Revelation to defend the position.[21]

Although this Midtribulation Rapture occurs at a separate time from the Second Coming, and *presumably* precedes God pouring out His wrath, the issue of the Church remaining on earth at the same time as Antichrist still remains. Scripturally, this is addressed above and in the previous chapter (7) by 2 Thessalonians 2:6–7: "And you know what restrains him (Antichrist) now, so that in his time he may be revealed…only he who now restrains will do so until he is taken out of the way." Traditionally, the "what" and "he" in these verses refer to the Body of Christ (Church), spoken of in the masculine gender by Paul in 1 Corinthians 12 and Ephesians 4.[22] Also, the issue of the Day of the Lord being narrowed down to just the latter part of the seven-year period goes against the body of research which relates the Day of the Lord to the entire Seven-year Tribulation Period (see chap. 7). Therefore, the midtribulational view seems to lack the cohesive and consistent testimony of the whole counsel of Scripture and also appears to be untenable.

There is also a "Partial Rapture Theory." This theory is based on such scriptures as Luke 21:36 and Matthew 25:1–13 (complemented by the wording in Phil 3:20; 2 Tim 4:8; Titus 2:13; and Heb 9:28). The theory states that only those Christians (or members of the Body of Christ/Church Universal) who are "eagerly" (diligently) "watching and waiting" (prepared), or "faithful" will be raptured. The prime example being the five prepared virgins of the "ten virgins" of Matthew 25. As such, this theory definitely separates out Christians who have reached some higher level of "spiritual attainment" from those who have not.[23] The whole premise of this theory goes against everything discussed above regarding the Rapture of the Church (the entire historical, universal Body of Christ or Church from the entire two thousand-year Church History) and makes the additional requirement that one must do something to earn the privilege to be part of the Rapture of the Church. That requirement totally goes against the orthodox understanding of becoming a

Christian (member of the Body of Christ) in the first place—salvation by God's grace through faith, a gift from God, not by human works, less anyone may boast (Eph 2:8–9). So, this Partial Rapture Theory must also be rejected.

Therefore, it appears that after considering all the views of when the Rapture of the Church is to take place, the Pretribulation Rapture of the Church (in complete fulfillment of the Perfect/Complete Gospel of Both Comings of Jesus Christ) holds the most scriptural and contextual credence. The next chapter will address the intermediate and final states of one's soul, and related judgments and resurrections. Another name for this is "Personal or Individual Eschatology."

9.

What Is Individual or Personal Eschatology?

The Intermediate State, Eternal State, and Associated Resurrections and Judgments

This chapter will address the Intermediate State, Eternal State, and associated Resurrections and Judgments of human beings. This is also known as Personal or Individual Eschatology—what happens after an individual's life ends or one dies. But before we can address Personal Eschatology, we need to delve a bit more into the concepts of death and the "Immortality of the Soul."

Before we enter into the discussion regarding death and the soul, there needs to be a short discussion about the varying views of the makeup of a human being, or theological anthropology, involving the terms "spirit," "soul," and "body."[1] The spirit is defined as, "the dimension of human life that enables a relationship with God."[2] The soul is defined as a human being's "life principle,"[3] or that part of humanity that consciously senses things, by perceiving, reflecting, feeling, and desiring.[4] And the body is defined as the "physical body of a person which is susceptible to death, and theologically, to the power of sin." Another name for the body theologically is "the flesh."[5] So theologically, the make-up of a human being is comprised of a combination of these three terms. Thrichotomism, or being tripartite, refers to the threefold nature of humanity as being made up of spirit, soul, and body.[6]

However, since the spirit is the human component that relates to God, and as a result of the Original Sin (or the Fall) of Adam and Eve in the Garden of Eden, each human being is born being spiritually "dead" (Gen 2:17; 3:17–19; Rom 5:12–16; 6:23; 1 Cor 15:21–22). And so, each person awaits being "born again," by spiritual regeneration or becoming a "new creation in Christ Jesus" (John 3:3–7; Rom 3:20–30; 10:8–13; 2 Cor 5:14b–18a). The Old Testament equivalent to this is being in covenant with God, accessed by grace through faith (Rom 4; 9; Heb 11), and looking forward to the coming of the Messiah (Christ in Greek). Dichotomism, or being bipartite, refers to the twofold nature of humanity as being made of spirit, soul, and body, with spirit and soul being "synonymous terms."[7] Monism, or being monistic, refers to humanity as not being made up of parts, but being whole, or a "radical unity" of spirit, soul, and body (again with spirit and soul being synonymous terms).[8] For the purposes of this discussion and moving forward, the tripartite description of humanity will be used (per 1 Thess 5:23), especially from a Christian perspective, with the human spirit component being made alive by the Holy Spirit at the new birth.

Moving on, a basic theological definition for death is, the "separation of the physical body from the soul." Another way to say this is, the termination of physical life by separation of the soul from the physical body (see Gen 2:7; Eccl 12:7; Matt 10:28; Jas 2:26).[9] Also speaking theologically, physical death is a result of the separation of humanity from God that occurred in Genesis 3—the Original Sin (Fall) of Adam and Eve, which led to *spiritual death immediately* and *ultimately physical death* (see Gen 2:17; 3:17–19; Rom 5:12–16; 6:23; 1 Cor 15:21–22).[10] Thus, when a person dies, his or her body goes back to the dust of the ground (decomposes per Gen 3:19), and his or her soul goes somewhere in the spiritual world (non-physical dimension per Eccl 12:7). The question then remains: Does that person's soul go to be eternally "with" or "separated from" God? This, in turn, brings up the issue of the "immortal soul."

For continuity's sake, the definition of the immortal soul, in light of death defined above, is as follows: at the end of the physical (natural) body, the soul lives on.[11] There are many scriptures in both the Old and New Testaments that give witness to the concept of an immortal soul from different perspectives. First we will address the Old Testament, and then, the New Testament scriptures. In Ecclesiastes 3:11, Solomon states that "He [God] has made everything appropriate in its time. He has also set eternity in their [humanity's] heart." In relation to Sheol (the place of the dead in the Old Testament), David mentions in Psalms 16:10 and 49:14–15 that the soul will not die. In Leviticus 19:31 and 20:27; Deuteronomy 18:11; and Isaiah 8:19 and 29:4, the Israelites were told not to communicate with the spirits of the dead or "familiar spirits." There are also scriptures that speak of humanity's communion with God in His eternal, spiritual world: Job 19:25–7 and Psalms 16:9–11, 17:5, and 73:23–4, 26. Finally, and interestingly enough, there are Old Testament scriptures that address the resurrection of the body to rejoin the soul (or spirit): Exodus 3:6; Job 19:23–27; Psalms 16:9–11, 17:15, and 49:15; Isaiah 26:19; and Daniel 12:2.[12] Next, the New Testament scriptures will be covered.

The key scripture of the New Testament regarding the immortality of the soul comes to light through Paul in 2 Timothy 1:10: "but now has been revealed by the appearing of our Savior Christ Jesus, who abolished death and *brought life and immortality to light through the gospel* [emphasis added]…"[13] Specifically, there are those scriptures that speak of the survival of the soul. For believers, they are: 1) Jesus referring to killing the body, but not the soul (Matt 10:28); 2) Jesus saying to the thief on the cross, "today you will be with me in paradise" (Luke 23:43); 3) Jesus saying to Martha, Lazarus' sister, that "he who believes in Me shall live even if he dies, and *everyone who lives and believes in Me shall never die* [emphasis added]" (John 11:25); and 4) Paul speaking of the "Judgment Seat of Christ" for believers after death in 2 Corinthians 5:10.

Then for unbelievers, they are: 1) Matthew 11:21–24 and 12:41, where Jesus speaks of the judgment day for unbelievers; and 2) Romans 2:5–11, where Paul also speaks of judgment of both believers and unbelievers. And, there are also those scriptures that speak of the soul in conjunction with the resurrected body: 1) Luke 20:35–36, where Jesus addresses "the Sadducees (who say there is no resurrection)" about marriage after death; 2) John 5:28–29, where Jesus speaks of the "resurrection of life" and the "resurrection of judgment" (see also Acts 24:15); 3) 1 Corinthians 15:20–54, where Paul speaks of the resurrection of believers and the "resurrection body" being like Jesus' resurrection body (see also Phil 3:21); and 4) 1 Thessalonians 4:13–18, where Paul speaks of the resurrection and Rapture of the Church (see previous chapter). Also in Revelation 20:6, 12–15, John speaks of the resurrection of unbelievers (or "wicked") as the "second death" or eternal death. And finally, as in the Old Testament, there are New Testament scriptures that talk of the believers communing with God in the Kingdom of God: Matthew 13:43; 25:34; Romans 2:7, 10; 1 Corinthians 15:44; Philippians 2:31; 2 Timothy 4:8; and Revelation 21:4 and 22:3–4.[14] With this as a basis for understanding life after death, we will now turn to the Intermediate State of the soul (soul and spirit for believers).

The Intermediate State can be defined as "the place of residence of the soul between death and resurrection of the body."[15] Please refer to the previous chapter for a complete discussion on the concept of resurrection, and specifically, the resurrection and Rapture of the Church. The easy explanation for the Intermediate State for believers and unbelievers is as follows:

1) For believers, their souls go to be in the presence of God; and 2) For unbelievers, their souls go a place separated from the presence of God, both awaiting the "resurrection of the dead."

Theologically, however, we must expound on this from a biblical and historical perspective. The best biblical picture of this separation of believers and unbelievers in the Intermediate State is given to us by Jesus in Luke 16:19–31, by the Story of the Rich Man and Lazarus. The understanding of this story is based on the Old Testament (Jewish) understanding of the departed souls/spirits of all people going to a place called Sheol.[16] In this story, both Lazarus and the Rich Man die, and their souls/spirits go to this concept of Sheol. *But, they are separated by "a great chasm fixed"* [emphasis added] *between the believers and unbelievers* (16:26): Lazarus (the believer) goes to "Abraham's Bosom" (Luke 16:22); and the Rich Man (unbeliever) goes to "Hades…being in torment" (16:23).

Theologically speaking, Abraham's Bosom can be interpreted in two ways: 1) as going directly to the presence of God—Heaven—from an Old Testament/Covenant perspective; or 2) as a temporary holding area for Old Testament saints until Jesus' Atonement, when Jesus took them all to Heaven with Him (Eph 4:9–10). This then is probably the picture of the Intermediate State of believers under the Old Covenant. The rest of the New Testament talks about Christians going to the presence of Christ when they die (Luke 23:43; 1 Cor 15:35–55; 2 Cor 5:1, 8; Phil 1:23; 1 Thess 4:13; 5:10; Heb 12:23; 1 Pet 3:18, 22). This place is generally referred to as "Heaven," but also "Paradise" by Jesus in Luke 23:43 and Paul in 2 Corinthians 12:3–4.[17]

Taking the same story in Luke 16 above, and expounding on the unbeliever's Intermediate State, the Rich Man goes to "Hades." The term Hades is the place where departed wicked souls/spirits go (Matt 11:23; 16:18; Luke 10:15; 16:23; Rev 1:18;

6:8; 20:13–14). In the New Testament, the term Hades is synonymous with Hell (Matt 22:13; 23:15, 33; Jude 13) and Gehenna (Matt 5:29–30; 10:28; 18:8–9; Mark 9:43, 45, 47; Luke 12:5).[18] This clearly shows the separation of believers' souls in God's presence from the unbelievers' souls in Hades/ Hell while in the Intermediate State.

The historical basis from Church History for the Intermediate State is testified to by the following Early Church Fathers and Catholic, Reformation, and Post-Reformation scholars, theologians, and preachers: Irenaeus (ca. AD 125–202); Clement of Rome (ca. 1st century AD); Ignatius (d. ca. AD 110); Justin Martyr (ca. AD 100–165); Athenagoras (ca. 2nd century AD); Origen (ca. AD 185–254); Methodius (ca. AD 260–311); John of Damascus (676–754); Thomas Aquinas (1225–1274); Martin Luther (1483–1546); John Calvin (1509–1564); Jonathan Edwards (1703–1758); and Charles Spurgeon (1834–1892).[19] Next, we will look at the resurrections and judgments at the conclusion of the Intermediate State.

As mentioned above, the Intermediate State ends with associated resurrections and judgments, which in turn, lead to each person's Eternal or Final State. These resurrections and judgments occur during the *Parousia*, or all the events surrounding the Second Coming of Jesus (see chapter 5). The biblical basis for these resurrections and judgments starts with Daniel 12:1–2: "Now at that time ["the time of the end"—Dan 11:40]…there will be a time of distress such as never occurred since there was a nation until that time; and at that time *your people*, everyone who is found written in the book [the "Book of Life"] will be rescued. *Many of those who sleep in the dust of the ground will awake, these to everlasting life, but the others to disgrace and everlasting contempt*" [emphasis added]. Here again, there can be seen the distinction between the resurrection and judgment of believers and unbelievers. But here, this scripture passage is speaking exclusively of Daniel's people ("your people"), the Jews.

In the New Testament, these concepts of resurrection and judgment are addressed by: Jesus Himself in Matthew 24:31–51 and 25; Paul in 1 Corinthians 15:21–26, Romans 14:10–12, 1 Corinthians 3:11–15, and 2 Corinthians 5:10; the writer of Hebrews in 9:27; and John in Revelation 7:9–17, 11:1–12, 14:1–5, and 20:4–6, 11–15. Next, we will look at each of these individually, to determine to whom each scripture refers, and when the resurrections and/or judgments will take place in the eschatological timeline of events. The following is a brief review of the order of events surrounding Jesus' Second Coming addressed by this book:

1) The Rapture of the Church (1 Thess 4:13–18; 1 Cor 15:51–55);

2) The Antichrist enters into a covenant with Israel for seven years and the Day of the Lord/Tribulation (divided into two 3½-year periods) ensues (Dan 9:27; 12:1–2, 11–12; Rev 4–18), ending with the Battle of Armageddon (Rev 14:14–20; 16:16; 19:17–19);

3) Jesus comes back to earth physically and visibly—on the Mount of Olives (Zech 14:4)—in great power and glory, with the Antichrist, False Prophet, and their entire army being destroyed (and the Antichrist and False Prophet being thrown into the Lake of Fire—their eternal/final state) (Rev 19:19–21);

4) Satan/the devil is bound for one thousand years, during which time, Jesus reigns on the earth in the Millennial/Messianic Kingdom (with resurrected saints judging, ruling, and reigning with Jesus) (Rev 20:1–6);

5) At the end of the Millennium, Satan is released for a short time, deceives more people to follow him against Jesus again, is defeated, judged, and also thrown into the Lake of Fire (Rev 20:7–10);

6) The Great White Throne Judgment takes place (Rev

20:11–15), which is specifically described below;

7) God creates a "New Heaven and New Earth," and both believers and unbelievers enter into their final/eternal states (Rev 21–22), which is also specifically described below.

Now, we will look at all the scriptures mentioned above.

Hebrews 9:27–28 acts as the overarching thematic scripture to begin with: "And inasmuch as *it is appointed for men to die once and after this comes judgment* [emphasis added], so Christ also, having been offered once to bear the sins of many, will appear a second time for salvation without reference to sin, to those who eagerly await Him." Next, Paul generally deals with the order of resurrections in 1 Corinthians 15:23–26: "But *each in his own order*: *Christ the first fruits, after that those who are Christ's at His coming, then comes the end* [emphasis added], when He hands over the kingdom to the God and Father, when He has abolished all rule and all authority and power. For He must reign until He has put all His enemies under His feet. The last enemy that will be abolished is death." So in simple terms, the order of resurrections occurs as follows:

1) Jesus at His First Coming (nearly two thousand years ago);

2) Believers at Jesus' *Parousia*/Second Coming (when exactly, to be determined below);

3) Unbelievers at "the end" of the Millennium, at the Great White Throne Judgment.

Next, we will look specifically at when the resurrections and judgments take place during the *Parousia*, using the remaining scriptures above.

First we must deal with the resurrection of the dead in Christ and the transformation of the living in Christ that takes place at the Rapture of the Church (1 Cor 15:35–55; 1 Thess 4:13–18), since this is the first event on the eschatological calendar. The judgment associated with the Rapture of the Church is called "the Judgment Seat of Christ" or the "*Bema* Seat Judgment," named for the word used in Greek for this in Romans 14:10 and 2 Corinthians 5:10. More fully explained by Romans 14:10–12, 1 Corinthians 3:11–15, and 2 Corinthians 5:10, this judgment will: take place following the Rapture of the Church, in Heaven, to include rewards and blessings only (since all punishment, condemnation, and curses were dealt with by Jesus at the cross), and to be followed by the "Marriage Supper of the Lamb" (Rev 19:7–8) in Heaven.[20] Remember, since the Rapture of the Church only applies to the Christians over the entire approximately two thousand-year history of the Church (Body of Christ), the Judgment Seat of Christ only applies to these Christians.

Next, by reading Matthew 24:31 – 25:46 first, followed by Revelation 20:1–6, then interspersing Revelation 7:9–17; 14:1–5; 11:1–12, and finishing with Revelation 20:11–15, we can come up with the following specific order of resurrections and associated judgments. This all begins immediately after Jesus' Second Coming (described by Matt 24:30 and Rev 19:11–21), in Matthew 24:31: "And He will send forth His angels with a great trumpet and they will gather together His elect from the four winds, from one end of the sky to the other." This then continues with Revelation 20:4–6:

> Then I saw thrones, and they sat on them, and judgment was given to them. And I saw the souls of those who had been beheaded because of their testimony of Jesus and because of the word of God, and those who had not worshiped the beast or his image, and had not received the mark on their forehead and on their hand; and they came to life and reigned with Christ for a thousand years. The rest of the dead did not come to life until the thousand years were completed. This is the *first resurrection*. Blessed and holy is the one who has a part in the *first resurrection*; over these the *second death* [emphasis added] has no power, but they will

be priests of God and of Christ and will reign with Him for a thousand years."

By combing these two scriptures and adding in Matthew 24:32–50 (including Matt 25:1–13, 14–30, and 31–46, describing three separate groups of people) and Revelation 7:9–17; 14:1–5; 11:1–12 (describing the Mid-Tribulation Rapture of Saints, the Rapture of the 144,000, and the resurrection and Rapture of the Two Witnesses), we can see the resurrections and/or associated judgments subsequent to the Rapture of the Church as follows:

> 1) The Old Testament Saints are resurrected and judged first (probably using the same criteria as the Judgment Seat of Christ) (Matt 24:31; 25:1–13).
>
> 2) Next, there will be all the Tribulation Saints who were martyred (Rev 6:9–11; 20:4) or were raptured (Rev 7:9–17; 11:1–12; 14:1–5) during the Tribulation (again, probably the same criteria as the Judgment Seat of Christ).
>
> 3) And finally, there are the *living Jews* first of Matthew 25:14–30, and then, "all the nations" (*living Gentiles*) of Matthew 25:31–46, who survived the Tribulation and will be judged by Jesus. The living believers repopulate the earth in the Millennial Kingdom, and the unbelievers are judged and sent to their Intermediate States, awaiting their resurrection and final judgment at the end of the Millennium at the Great White Throne Judgment.
>
> 4) During and after the Millennium, but before the Great White Throne Judgment, anyone who dies will presumably be judged on the spot, and given the appropriate judgment (and resurrection, if a believer).
>
> 5) Finally, the Great White Throne Judgment occurs for all unbelievers at the end of the Millennium (Rev 20:11–15).[21]

This then leads to the Final or Eternal States for both believers and unbelievers. The first mention of the Eternal State for unbelievers (Lake of Fire) is in Matthew 25:41 ("eternal fire prepared for Satan and his angels"). This is confirmed by Jesus in Mark 9:43–49 (although reference to "everyone will be salted with fire" in verse 49 explains the unbeliever in Hell and the believer at the Judgment Seat of Christ). See also Jude 6 (speaking of the angels who procreated with women in Gen 6:2–5; 2 Pet 2:4), Jude 7 (speaking of Sodom, Gomorrah, and surrounding cities as examples of unbelievers' "punishment of eternal fire"), and Revelation 19:20b (Beast/False Prophet thrown into Lake of Fire). After the Millennium of Revelation 20:1–6, there remain two judgments related to the Eternal State of unbelievers:

> 1) Satan is released for a short time, and gathers another army from the nations against God's holy people and Jerusalem (Armageddon II), fire comes from heaven, destroys the army, and Satan is thrown into the Lake of Fire (Rev 20:7–10);

> 2) The Great White Throne Judgment is conducted by God the Father for all dead unbelievers (Rev 20:11–15): "Books" will be opened and also the "Lamb's Book of Life" or "Book of Life." Unbelievers are then judged by their deeds and if their names are written in the Book of Life (*presumably they are not*); and then, their Eternal State is the Lake of Fire (the "second death"—Rev 20:14).[22] (Note that the Book of Life is also mentioned in Exod 32:32–33; Deut 29:20; Pss 69:28 and 139:16; Dan 12:1; Luke 10:20; Phil 4:3; Heb 12:23; and Rev 3:5; 13:8–9; 17:8; 21:27; 22:19. It appears from all these Scripture passages that every human being born is recorded in the Book of Life and remains there until death; at which time, his or her name either remains in the Book of Life [believers], or is "blotted out" or "erased" from it [unbelievers]).

Next, we will address the Eternal State of believers.

The Eternal State for believers is clearly, specifically, and gloriously spelled out by Revelation 21–22. A New Heaven and New Earth are created by God, including a New Jerusalem, prepared for the Eternal State of believers (Rev 21:1–8). Then, a specific description is given of the New Jerusalem. Geographically, its length, width, and height are fifteen hundred miles (Rev 21:16). Its walls are seventy-two yards thick (21:17). It has twelve gates for the Twelve Tribes of Israel (21:12) and twelve foundation stones for the Twelve Apostles of Jesus (21:14). There is no Temple in it, because "the Lord God, the Almighty and the Lamb, are its temple" (21:22). A river of the "water of life" flows from God's throne in the center of it, watering the "tree of life" (22:1–2, and reminiscent of the river and tree of life in the Garden of Eden—Gen 2:9–10). And eternally, there will be no more curse, death, nor night (22:3–5). Thus in this Eternal State for believers: *chronos* time stops, and *kairos* time supersedes it into eternity; God's original intent at creation for His kingdom on earth for humanity is realized; and fellowship between God and humanity is restored for all eternity.[23]

On a separate (and very minor) side note: There is an *unorthodox and unbiblical belief that will not be addressed by this book regarding the Eternal State of all humanity (no distinction between believers and unbelievers): Universalism* (which teaches that everyone goes to be with God in Heaven, when they die). Following that, there are *two separate unbiblical and unorthodox beliefs* which will be addressed next: one regarding *the Eternal State of unbelievers (Annihilationism)*; and one regarding *the Intermediate State of believers (Purgatory)*.

Annihilationism is the belief that the wicked (unbelievers) will not be allowed to suffer a Final State (eternity) in a conscious Hell; but after their final judgment, they will be "annihilated," or cut off from existence (like they never existed at all). This belief is also called Conditional Immortality. Theologians who hold to this belief (although very few in number) state that this view aligns closer with God's mercy, and that certain selected scriptures addressing the Final State of Unbelievers (e.g., Pss 21:9, 37:28, 55:23, 92:7, and 145:2; Mal 4:1, 3; Matt 10:28), especially the "second death" of Revelation 2:11; 20:6, 14, and 21:8, seem to indicate the cessation of the immortal soul (i.e., the first death is the normal physical death of a person, and the second death is the death of one's soul). But since this whole line of reasoning goes against the previous discussion of the immortal soul; was condemned as heresy by most orthodox teachers in Church History, the Athanasian Creed, and several Ecumenical Church Councils of the Early Church; and lacks sound biblical exegesis and hermeneutics for proper interpretation of scripture, Annihilationism cannot be accepted as a viable option for the Eternal State for unbelievers.[24]

Purgatory is an Intermediate State doctrine for believers, primarily believed by Roman Catholics, many Anglicans, and some Eastern Orthodox, and which can best be defined as "a period of temporal punishment for sins after death and before heaven." These sins are unremitted (unrepented) *venial* sins (lesser, easier to forgive sins) versus *mortal* sins. Although some scripture passages are given as "indirect references" to Purgatory (Matt 5:26; 12:32; and 1 Cor 3:15; and 2 Maccabees 12:42–46 in the *Apocrypha* of the Catholic Bible), the primary defense for the doctrine is from the tradition of Early Church Latin Fathers (such as Cyprian [AD 200–258] and Augustine [AD 354–430]) and "theological speculation." Also, this doctrine of dealing with certain sins after death seems to directly contradict the complete Atonement for sins accomplished by Jesus' death, burial, and resurrection. Therefore, based on the above, brief treatment of the subject, and specifically the lack of direct biblical evidence for it, Purgatory cannot be accepted as a viable option for the Intermediate State of believers.[25] Therefore, after treating all the issues related to Personal

Eschatology, the next chapter will discuss the "Signs of the Times," or how close we appear to be to the *Parousia* of Jesus.

10.

Signs of the Times

How Close Are We to the Rapture of the Church?

Many of the "signs of the times" have been singularly addressed by previous chapters of this book. Therefore, this chapter is provided to gather them all together in one place, fill in the gaps, and place them in a logical order. This process should show the increasing number, frequency, and intensity of these signs and "birth pains" (Matt 24:8; Mark 13:8). And, this should also hopefully show how close the Body of Christ may be to the "Blessed Hope" (Titus 2:13) of the *Parousia* (the Rapture of the Church that precedes the Second Coming of the Lord Jesus Christ—see chapter 8). Additionally, knowing this should encourage Christians around the world to once again raise up the standard and proclaim the Perfect/Complete Gospel of Both Comings of Jesus Christ. The biblical timelines addressed in chapter 3 will be used as starting points to highlight various overarching prophetic signs established by God in Genesis and Daniel. Next, those prophetic signs in those timelines which have been fulfilled to date will be explored. Then, other specific Old Testament prophetic signs, related to these timelines that have been fulfilled, will be considered. Finally, the outline of the "birth pains" and signs addressed by Jesus Himself in the Apocalyptic Discourse (Matt 24; Mark 13; and Luke 21), that have been fulfilled, are about to be fulfilled, or yet to be fulfilled, will be addressed.

As alluded to in chapter 3, it was a common understanding

of the Early Church that God used the "Creation Week" in Genesis 1, coupled with the notion of "a day with the Lord is as a thousand years" (Ps 90:4; 2 Pet 3:8), as a pattern for a chronology of humanity's lease on earth as six thousand years. This then will lead up to the seventh day or "sabbath rest" of one thousand years of the Millennial Kingdom.[1] This being the overarching premise of all the prophetic signs to come elicits a beginning point for the timeline. As also addressed by chapter 3 above, some theologians believe that the year 2019 corresponds to the year 5779 per the Jewish calendar; to the year 6023 per the best combined estimates from the Julian, Gregorian, and Bishop Ussher's calendars;[2] and to the year 6019–6020 per Michael Rood's newly discovered Astronomically and Agriculturally Corrected Biblical Hebrew Calendar.[3] Thus, the beginning point of this calendar is roughly 4,000 BC.

This overarching timeline may then be broken down into the following subtimelines: 1) the Seven Old Testament Feasts and their prophetic fulfillments; 2) Israel's Timeline from Daniel 9 and 12, and Hosea 5–6; and 3) the Gentile's Timeline from Daniel 2, 7, 8, and 10–11. And, all these subtimelines contain a **gap** that represents the Church Age or Times of the Gentiles (Luke 21:24; John 4:34–38; 21:22–23; Rom 11:25; Rev 2–3; and Rev 11:2). The Church Age/Times of the Gentiles begins with Jesus' ascension (Rapture), and ends with the corresponding Rapture of the Church (Body of Christ) per chapter 8 of this book. These subtimelines will now be addressed one by one.

The seven Old Testament Feasts (Passover, Unleavened Bread, Firstfruits, Weeks/Pentecost, Trumpets, Atonement, and Booths/Tabernacles), which are addressed in chapter 3, were established by God in concert with the Mosaic Covenant (which included the sabbath day of rest to honor God for His creation and provision). They were to be annual, recurring, covenant

Sabbaths in remembrance of His faithfulness, grace, and provision to His people (Lev 23). Additionally, God instituted a "Sabbatical Year/Jubilee" concept (which marked off seven, seven-year cycles, culminating with the fiftieth year being the Year of Jubilee), to remind His chosen people that the earth/land was His and that He made it (Lev 25).

Passover, Unleavened Bread, Firstfruits, and Weeks/Pentecost occur in the spring. Separated by approximately four months, Trumpets, Atonement, and Booths/Tabernacles occur in the autumn. Of these seven feasts, God required the males of Israel to appear before Him at the Tabernacle (or later, the Temple) three times a year: Unleavened Bread, Weeks/Pentecost, and Booths/Tabernacles—at the beginning, middle, and end of the year (Deut 16:16). In addition to reminding Israel of their relationship/covenant with God, these feasts also served to prophetically foreshadow future events on God's timeline for His chosen people. *The first three feasts were fulfilled by Jesus Christ's death, burial, and resurrection*: *Passover*—Matthew 26:2/John 19:14/1 Corinthians 5:7; *Unleavened Bread*—Mark 14:22/John 6:51/1 Corinthians 10:16; and *Firstfruits*—Mark 16:1–6/John 20:1, 19–23/1 Corinthians 15:20–23. The *Feast of Weeks/Pentecost was fulfilled by the birth/empowerment of the Church*, addressed in Acts 1:1–5; 2:1–4. This was then followed by the **gap** in the timeline (**the Church Age/Times of the Gentiles**). Thus, the *Feast of Trumpets* should be fulfilled at the end of the Church Age/Times of the Gentiles by the *Rapture of the Church* (Luke 21:36; 1 Thess 4:16–17; Rev 4:1; 7:9–18; 12:5—see chap. 8). Following this "Blessed Hope" of the Church (Body of Christ) remains the *Feast of Atonement*, which should be fulfilled when God judges humanity and the earth for their sins on the Day of the Lord or the Seven-year Tribulation Period (Matt 24:9–22; Rev 5–19—see chap. 7); and the *Feast of Booths/Tabernacles*, which should be fulfilled during the millennial reign of King Jesus (Isa 9:6–7; Ezek

40–48; Joel 3:18–21; Zeph 3:8–20; Zech 14:4–21; Mic 4:1–5; Rev 20:2–4—see chap. 6).[4]

Israel's Timeline, as mentioned in Daniel 9:24–27; 12 (and in chapter 3 above), and confirmed by Hosea 5:14–6:3, consists of seventy weeks of years (70 x 7, or 490 years, from the "sabbatical year" concept). The purposes of these sabbath years were to: 1) finish the transgression (began at Jesus' First Coming and to be completed at His Second Coming); 2) make an end of sin (began at Jesus' First Coming and to be completed at His Second Coming); 3) make atonement for iniquity (fulfilled at Jesus' First Coming); 4) bring in everlasting righteousness (began at Jesus' First Coming and to be completed at His Second Coming); 5) seal up vision and prophecy (to be fulfilled at Jesus' Second Coming); and 6) anoint the Most Holy Place (began at Jesus' First Coming and to be completed at His Second Coming)—Daniel 9:24.

Of these 490 years, 483 years were to be from the decree issued to restore and rebuild Jerusalem until "Messiah the Prince is cut off" (Dan 9:25–26). This was literally fulfilled from the decree of Artaxerxes in 445–444 BC (Neh 2:1–10) to Jesus' death on the cross in AD 31–33 (factoring in the Gregorian calendar being off by approximately two to four years, miscalculating the year of Jesus' birth, and the transition from BC to AD). Next, "the prince who is to come" (Dan 9:26) was to destroy Jerusalem and the Temple. This was fulfilled by General Titus (son of Emperor Vespasian) and his Roman legion in AD 70.

Then, there remains the "gap" of the "Times of the Gentiles," until "he [Antichrist] will make a firm covenant with the many for one week" (Dan 9:27), or seven years; "but in the middle of the week he will put a stop to sacrifice and grain offering; and on the wing of abominations will come one who makes desolate, even until a complete destruction, one that is decreed, is poured out on the one who makes desolate." The latter section of verse 27 is talking about Mid-Tribulation, when the Antichrist breaks the covenant with Israel, sets up the "Abomination of Desolation," destroys the world religious "harlot" (one-world religion of Rev 17:16–18), and declares himself to be God in the Temple (2 Thess 2:3–4), and the False Prophet starts the "mark of the Beast" (Rev 13:16–18) and idol worship (Rev 13:14–15). Then, the final 3½ years of the Tribulation are known as the Great Tribulation, concluded at the Battle of Armageddon by the Second Coming of Jesus.[5] See chapters 5–8 for more specific information on all these events.

Interwoven within Israel's Timeline remains an interesting prophecy contained in Hosea 5:14–6:3. This prophecy speaks of the Jews being "torn away" from *Yahweh*, and of Him "going away" and returning to His "place." Next, it gives encouragement in verse 6:1: "Come, let us return to the LORD. For He has torn us, but He will heal us; He has wounded us, but He will bandage us" (speaking of Messiah's First Coming). Then, comes the interesting part of the prophecy contained in verse 2 (and using the "day with the Lord = 1,000 years" analogy): "He will revive us after two days (two thousand years); He will raise us up on the third day (third 1,000 years) that we may live before Him." Interpreting it this way from a prophetic perspective, addresses the two thousand years of **the Times of the Gentiles/Church Age**, followed by the Millennium. This prophetic scripture has also been interpreted to speak of Messiah's being resurrected on the third day. While this scripture could have multiple fulfillments, it appears to be speaking of the nation of Israel and its relationship to *Yahweh*. Therefore, the first prophetic interpretation of the completion of the Church Age and the Millennium following appears to be the more valid one.[6]

The Gentiles' Timeline, mentioned in Daniel 2 and 7 and chapter 3 above, and more specifically broken down by Daniel

8, 10, and 11, is represented by Nebuchadnezzar's statue made of different materials and by the four beasts to arise out of the earth. Each metal (in decreasing order of value) and associated beast represents a kingdom that will rule over Israel. The "head of gold" and "lion with wings of an eagle" represent Nebuchadnezzar's Babylonian Empire (Dan 2:38; 7:4). The "breast and arms of silver," "bear raised up on one side with three ribs in its mouth," and "ram with two horns" represent the Medio-Persian Empire (Dan 2:39; 5:28; 7:5; 8:3–4, 20). The "belly and thighs of bronze," "leopard with four wings like a bird and four heads," and "shaggy goat with a conspicuous horn broken off and replaced with four horns" represent the Grecian Empire of Alexander the Great, broken into the four kingdoms of his four generals (Dan 2:39; 7:6; 8:5–8, 21–22; 10:20; 11:2–3).[7] The "legs of iron" and "fourth beast which was terrifying, extremely strong, and had large iron teeth" represent the Roman Empire (Dan 2:40; 7:7, 23). During the Roman Empire, and according to Daniel 9:26, "Messiah will be cut off and have nothing, [Jesus crucified in AD 31–33] and the people of the prince who is to come will destroy the city and the sanctuary" [General Titus and his Roman legion in AD 70].[8] After this, in AD 313, Emperor Constantine declared Christianity to be the religion of the Roman Empire.[9] And in 1054, the Roman Empire (and the Church) was eventually divided into the East (Constantinople) and West (Rome).[10] Then, there remains the **Church Age gap**.

This **gap** remains until the Rapture of the Church at its terminus and the rise of the Antichrist (Dan 9:27). At that time, the fifth and final kingdom made up of "the feet and toes of iron mixed with clay" and "ten horns on the fourth beast," which represent a Ten-Nation Confederacy from the confines of the Old Roman Empire, will arise, as addressed in Daniel 2:44; 7:7b–8, 24. Most dispensational theologians (including C. I. Scofield, Arno Gaebelein, J. Vernon McGee, Hal Lindsey, Jack Van Impe, Tim

LaHaye, Pat Robertson, and Noah W. Hutchings) believe this to be ten nations from the European Economic Community/Union (old Common Market).[11] However, recent studies by Colin Deal and J. R. Church declare it to be an Arab/Muslim Ten-Nation Confederacy, based on those nations described as enemies of Israel and seeking to destroy it as a nation outlined by Psalm 83 (vv. 4–5: "They have said, 'Come, and let us wipe them out as a nation, That the name of Israel be remembered no more.' For they have conspired together with one mind; Against You they make a covenant..."). These ten Old Testament nations (Edom, the Ishmaelites, Moab, the Hagrites/Hagarenes, Gebal, Ammon, Amalek, Philistia/the Philistines, Tyre, and Assyria/Assur—vv. 6–8) make up parts of, or all, of the following modern Arab countries that surround Israel: Jordan, Saudi Arabia, Kuwait, Iraq, Egypt, Lebanon, the Palestinians (PLO), Syria, Iran, and Turkey.[12] Most parts of these modern nations fall within the confines of the Old Roman Empire.[13] And, all but Iran and Turkey are part of the Arab League (founded in 1945), *whose explicit, first and foremost, goal is the destruction of Israel.*[14] In light of this study's information, the world events occurring in the Middle East since the close of WWII, and the meteoric rise of Radical Islamic Terrorism and Islam as a major world religion since 9/11/2001, it appears that the Ten-Nation Arab Confederacy (from Psalm 83) is the more likely choice for fulfillment of Daniel's fifth kingdom made partly of iron and partly of clay.

In Daniel 8, this Gentile timeline has additional specific prophecies pertaining to the partitioning of the Grecian Empire after Alexander the Great's death (at the age of 32)[15] into "four horns" (v. 8) by his top four generals. Then, "out of one of them came forth a rather small horn," representing "a king [who] will arise...in the latter period of their rule," who will desecrate "the holy place" (the Second Temple) and stop the "regular sacrifice...for 2,300 evenings and mornings" (vv. 9,

11–14). Then in Daniel 11, the "four horns" of Daniel 8 are further clarified to be "parceled out toward the four points of the compass" (v.4—Lysimachus "took Thrace and much of Asia Minor"; Cassander took "Macedonia and Greece"; Ptolemy took "Egypt, Palestine, Cilicia, Petra, and Cyprus…beginning the Ptolemaic Dynasty in Egypt which lasted until the death of Cleopatra VII in 31" BC; and Seleucus "took…the rest of Asia…founding the Seleucid Empire which was comprised of Syria, Babylon, Persia, and India").[16]

The Northern Kingdom (the Seleucids of Syria) and the Southern Kingdom (the Ptolemies of Egypt) then engage in many battles and wars in a struggle for power in Daniel 11. This ends with a Syrian king fulfilling the prophecy in Daniel 8 about the "small horn" desecrating the Temple and stopping the "regular sacrifice…for 2,300 evenings and mornings." This is further clarified in Daniel 11:31, to be when he puts "a stop to the daily sacrifices" and sets up "the abomination of desolation" in the "sanctuary." This specific prophecy was fulfilled by Antiochus IV (Epiphanes) during his reign between 175–164 BC (most probably 167–164 BC, counting both the evening and morning sacrifices occurring in one day, thus, dividing the 2,300 into 1,150 days).[17] Then, the prophecy in Daniel 11, goes on to speak of "the end time" (v. 40), *when one like Antiochus Epiphanes* will "enter the Beautiful Land, and many countries will fall…. But he will gain control over the hidden treasures of gold and silver…he will go forth with great wrath to destroy and annihilate many…. And he will pitch the tents of his royal pavilion between the seas and the beautiful Holy Mountain; yet he will come to his end and no one will help him" (vv. 41–45). This section of scripture is speaking of the Islamic Antichrist (see chapter 7)[18] who will arise at the time of the Ten-Nation Arab Confederacy.

Continuing with Daniel 12:1: "Now at that time Michael, the

great prince who stands guard over the sons of your people, will arise. And there will be a time of distress such as never occurred since there was a nation until that time…" (the *Great Tribulation*—see chapter 7). This Great Tribulation will last for 3½ years: "from the time that the regular sacrifice is abolished and the abomination of desolation is set up, there will be 1,290 days" (Dan 12:11). This is the same 3½ years spoken of in Dan 9:27: "in the middle of the week he will put a stop to sacrifice…." Note that *Daniel 12:1b–2 also speaks of the resurrection of the Old Testament Saints* (see chapter 9): "and at that time your people, everyone who is found written in the book, will be rescued. And many of those who sleep in the dust of the ground will awake, these to everlasting life, but the others to disgrace and everlasting contempt." Next, those additional specific prophecies from the Old Testament that support these subtimelines will be explored.

These prophecies are in addition to all the previously mentioned Old Testament prophecies about both the First and Second Comings of Jesus Christ, which were addressed in chapter 5. Continuing on, both Isaiah and Jeremiah speak of the city of Babylon, which will "never [be] inhabited again" (Isa 13:19–22; Jer 50:39–40; 51:37–43). Note that Saddam Hussein tried to rebuild it (resurrect it from out of the desert) in the 1980s/90s, but failed. Isaiah 47, Jeremiah 51:7, and Zechariah 5 speak of the "spirit of Babylon," "daughter of Babylon," or "Babylon the Harlot" (mentioned in Revelation 17 and 18), which is indicative of the Babylonian Mysteries Cult false-religious spirit present from the time of Nimrod (Gen 10:8–12; 11:1–9) and his wife Semiramis[19] throughout history until its end mentioned by Revelation 17:16–18.

The following prophecies speak of the regathering or rebirth of the nation of Israel. Isaiah 66:7–8 specifically addresses Israel being "born in a single day" (which occurred on May 14, 1948, when the new flag of the state of Israel reached the top of the flagpole).[20] Ezekiel 11:13–20; 20:33–44; and 36–7 (specifically, 37:15–28) conclude that Israel will be restored as "one nation again." Hosea 3:4–5 and Isaiah 27:6 declare that Israel will "take root and blossom and fill the earth with fruit." And, Amos 9:15 states that after the rebirth that Israel "will no more be uprooted from their Land."

On a separate eschatological note, Isaiah 19:19–20 speaks of there being "an altar to the LORD in the midst of the land of Egypt, and a pillar to the LORD near its border. It will become a sign and a witness to the LORD of hosts in the land of Egypt." This was fulfilled by understanding that the Great Pyramid of Giza was built by Enoch (Gen 5:21–23) before Noah and the Great Flood (Gen 6–9).[21] Also, Ezekiel, in his visions contained in 1:4–28 and 10:1–22, mentions the "Cherubim," who equate to the "four living creatures" of Revelation 4. Zechariah 6:1–8 mentions the "four horsemen of the Apocalypse" from Revelation 6. And, Zechariah 4 mentions the "two olive trees that stand before the LORD," which equate to the "Two Witnesses" of Revelation 11.

Chapter 7 addresses the Day of the LORD (*Yahweh*)/Jacob's Trouble prophecies that speak of the "Tribulation." However, the following citations deal specifically with the "Battle of Armageddon" (mentioned by name in Rev 16:16), which will occur at the end of the Tribulation and just prior to the Second Coming of Jesus: Ezekiel 39:1–24; Micah 4:11–13; Zechariah 14:1–6, 12–15. Zechariah 14:4 specifically states that "His feet" ("the LORD's," from verse 3) will physically "stand on the Mount of Olives." And finally, chapter 6 addresses the Millennial Kingdom prophecies.

Next, the New Testament "signs of the times" will be explored. The primary and overarching *sign* from the New Testament is the outline of the Church Age. It is broken into seven periods based on the names of the churches described in Revelation 2 and 3:

1) Ephesus (Rev 2:1–7): the Birth of the Church (approx. AD 33) to the destruction of the Jerusalem/the Temple (AD 70) and the Apostolic Fathers (approx. AD 100);

2) Smyrna (Rev 2:8–11): Period of Persecution (approx. AD 100 to AD 313—Constantine declaring Christianity the religion of the Roman Empire);

3) Pergamum (Rev 2:12–17): Rise of Heresies and Controversies (AD 313 to approx. AD 500);

4) Thyatira (Rev 2:18–29): First Pope to Rise of Islam to Church Split (East and West) (approx. AD 500 to 1054);

5) Sardis (Rev 3:1–6): Rise of Moslem Latin Avveroism, Scholasticism, Monasticism, the Crusades through the Middle Ages (1054 to 1517);

6) Philadelphia (Rev 3:7–13): Protestant Reformation, Bible type-printed and translated, Great Awakenings, Revivals, Missionaries sent out, and Pentecostal/Charismatic Movements (1517 to approx. 1960); and

7) Laodicea (Rev 3:14–22): Post-Modern Period begins—lukewarm, rich, with no need of anything (but really wretched, poor, blind, and naked), love grows cold, falling away (apostasy), deceiving spirits (Jude 11–13, 18–19; 1 Tim 4:1; 2 Tim 3:1; 2 Thess 2:3–4; Rev 3:20—last period before the end of the Church Age, and Jesus, who is standing at the door, returns for His Body)—(1960 to the Rapture of the Church).[22]

Then, there remains the Apocalyptic Discourse of Jesus in Matthew 24, Mark 13, and Luke 21.

The first prophetic sign mentioned by Jesus Christ Himself in Matthew 24:2, Mark 13:2, and primarily Luke 21:5–6, 20–24, signaling the beginning of the Last Days and the "Times of the Gentiles," was the destruction of Jerusalem and the Temple (fulfilled some forty years after He spoke the prophecy, in AD

70). Next, Jesus spoke of the persecution of the Early Church in Luke 21:12–19, which started under Nero (in AD 64)[23] and lasted until Constantine (AD 313).

Jesus then spoke of the following signs that would be like "the beginning of birth pangs," which would increase in frequency and intensity until the time of birth (His *Parousia*) in Matthew 24:4–8. The first sign is that "false Christs" would come and "mislead many" (v. 5). This started in the Early Church shortly after Jesus' ascension, has continued through the Church Age, has dramatically increased since 1948 (the rebirth of the Nation of Israel), and will conclude with the Antichrist (the false proclamation of Lord Maitreya in 1982 was the first attempt of Satan to bring him to the forefront).[24]

The second sign is "wars and rumors of wars" (v. 6). Wars have happened with increased frequency, especially the "rumors of wars" part, since the end of WWII, the second "war to end all wars," ending in 1945. This war was followed by the Korean Conflict (1950–1953), the Vietnam Conflict (1955–1975), the Six Day War in 1967, the *Yom Kippur* War in 1973, the First Gulf War in 1990–1991, the "War on Terror," following 9/11/2001—the Afghanistan War (2001–present), the Iraq War (2003–2011), and the wars/conflicts involving IS/ISIS in Iraq, Iran, Egypt, Libya, Pakistan, Lebanon, and Syria—and will continue until the Battle of Armageddon (Rev 16:12–16; 19:11–21).

The third sign is "nation against nation" and "kingdom against kingdom" (v. 7a). In addition to the wars described above, this has happened with increased frequency since WWII, not just in war, but financially, politically, and socially. Prime examples are the fall of Communism in Eastern Europe (1989) and in Russia (1991), and the resulting realignment and renaming of nations in Europe and Asia, the civil wars, internal conflicts, and subsequent renaming of African nations, and the solidifying of the Arab League against Israel as a nation (founded in Cairo in March 1945 with six members—Egypt, Iraq, Lebanon, Saudi Arabia, Syria, and Jordan—and now has 22 member states).[25] And, the fourth sign is "famines and earthquakes in various places" (v. 7b). Again, both earthquakes and famines have been increasing in frequency and intensity since recorded history in the thirteenth century, especially with the exponential world population increase and recent natural disasters that often accompany earthquakes, such as droughts, floods, volcanic eruptions, tsunamis, and hurricanes.[26]

After these signs have occurred, Jesus states in verses 9–10, "They will deliver you to tribulation and will kill you, and you will be hated by all nations on account of My name. And many will fall away and will deliver up one another." This happened initially during the persecution of the Early Church, was repeated in extreme measure to the Jews (God's chosen people) during the Holocaust of WWII, and recently in the era of Postmodernism has begun to happen to Christianity (especially related to "on account of My name"). Next, Jesus says in verses 10–11, "And many false prophets will arise, and will mislead many. And because lawlessness is increased, most people's love will grow cold." Again, this has exponentially increased, starting with the proliferation of cults and cultic personalities in the 1950s–60s, and leading to the postmodern, selfish era of New Age and Radical Islam.

Jesus then mentions more signs in Luke 21:25, "And there will be signs in the sun, moon, and stars, and upon the earth dismay among nations, in perplexity at the roaring of the sea and the waves, men fainting from fear and the expectation of the things which are coming upon the world; for the powers of the heavens will be shaken." Starting in 1982 (same year as Lord Maitreya was identified), all planets in the earth's solar system aligned on the same side of the sun, which coincided with the eleven-year sunspot cycle, causing increased natural disasters and strange weather patterns, and holes in the ozone layer have increased UV rays from the sun. In 1986, Haley's Comet returned with other comets, meteor showers, and increased UFO sightings. And recently, all the earthquakes, tsunamis, hurricanes, and terrorist attacks of the twenty-first century were combined into a worldwide event in the movie "2012" (30 years after 1982). Additionally, there has also been the increase of the Blood Moon phenomena (2014–present).[27] While there were seven deadly natural disasters in 2017,[28] in 2018 (70 years after Israel became a nation in 1948), there have been nineteen natural disasters,[29] and two blood moons.[30] This will culminate with what Jesus mentions in Matthew 24:29, "But immediately after the tribulation of those days the sun will be darkened, and the moon will not give its light, and the stars will fall from the sky, and the powers of the heavens will be shaken." This is confirmed by John's vision in Revelation 16:17–21 (the seventh bowl judgment).

The final sign Jesus mentions that will occur before the appearance of the Antichrist and the Tribulation is in Matthew 24:14 as follows: "And this *gospel of the kingdom shall be preached in the whole world for a witness to all the nations, and then the end shall come* [emphasis added]." **It is important to note that the Perfect/Complete Gospel of the Kingdom being preached in the whole world for a witness is the last sign to be fulfilled before the end**. This has been, and will continue to be done by the Church (Body of Christ), in accordance with the Great Commission in Matthew 28:18–20, until the Rapture of the Church. After that, during the Tribulation, the Holy Spirit will still be present on the earth to dispense God's grace, mercy, Word, and salvation through the 144,000 Jewish Witnesses of Revelation 7:1–8; 14:1–5; the Two Witnesses of Revelation 11; the angelic ministry of Revelation 14:6–20; and all those who become believers and also witness during the Tribulation.[31]

According to many Missions organizations, approximately 99% of the world's nations have heard the Gospel.[32] And according to Wycliffe Bible Translators, approximately 96% of the world has the Bible translated into their language, or it is in the process of being translated. Their vision, as an organization, is to have the task completed by the year 2025.[33] This then remains the final "sign of the times" as the world approaches the end of the Last Days and the completion of the **Times of the Gentiles/the Church Age**.

However after this, in Matthew 24:15–29, Jesus mentions various signs that will take place during the Seven-Year Tribulation (primarily focusing on "The day is coming when you will see what Daniel the prophet spoke about—the sacrilegious object that causes desecration standing in the Holy Place. [Reader, pay attention!]"—in verse 15). This then ends with verses 30–31 speaking about His Second Coming. The "Holy Place" mentioned in verse 15 is speaking of the rebuilt Temple (Third Temple in Jerusalem), and corresponds with "but in the middle of the week he will put a stop to sacrifice and grain offering; and on the wing of abominations will come one who makes desolate, even until a complete destruction, one that is decreed, is poured out on the one who makes desolate" in Daniel 9:27. This brings up the question of, "How close is Israel to building the Third Temple?"

Since being established in 1987, the Temple Institute in Jerusalem has been working on all the preparations to rebuild the Third Temple. Since then: the Orthodox Jews have reestablished the "Sanhedrin," the religious body that oversees the religious "(legal) issues related to the Temple." And specifically, they have: constructed "a cornerstone for the Third Temple"; made "all the ritual vessels necessary for the function of the Temple"; trained the priests for their "future work" in the Temple, including "reenactments of Temple ceremonies" conducted using ritual vessels and the "newly constructed Altar of Burnt Offering"; and are working to restore the sacred "ashes of the Red Heifer" of Numbers 19 for purification to Israel.[34] Also related to the rebuilding of the Third Temple was President Trump's recent Declaration of Jerusalem being the eternal capital of Israel and moving the U.S. Embassy to Jerusalem.[35]

Related to the articles necessary to complete the Temple, the only article behind the veil of the "Holy of Holies" is the Ark of the Covenant (Exod 25:10; 26:33–34; 40:3, 21). And according to 1 Kings 8:9, the Ark of the Covenant contains only the "the two stone tablets of the Ten Commandments." The Ark was in the First Temple (Solomon's Temple), but was removed from it before the Temple was destroyed by the Babylonians in 586 BC (2 Chr 36:17–20).[36] And when the Second Temple was built by Ezra in 515 BC (Ezra 6:14–15), "the Babylonian Talmud asserts that" the Ark was missing.[37] Since that time there have been many theories as to where the Ark may have been hidden (including Ethiopia, Egypt, Mt. Nebo in Jordan, or in Jerusalem near the Temple Mount). However, recent evidence has come to light that Ron Wyatt (1933–1999) may have discovered the hiding place of the Ark in "Jeremiah's Grotto," beneath Golgotha, the hill on which Jesus was crucified (outside of the Old City, in the Arab Quarter, north of the Temple Mount, out of the Damascus Gate, adjacent to the Garden Tomb).[38] But, after a January 2019 trip to Israel, and hearing a recording from the Director of the Temple Institute (Rabbi Chaim Richman),[39] talking to a Jewish archaeologist, who is in charge of the Western Wall tunnel excavations and expert on the Ark of the Covenant (Avraham Solomon, Ph.D.),[40] and receiving a disclaimer press release from the Garden Tomb Association,[41] it became clear that Wyatt's claims appeared to be proven false. Instead, there appears to be a very strong case from rabbinic teachings and historic archaeology (confirmed by Rabbi Getz and Rabbi Goren after the Six-Day War in 1967–1981) that the

Ark of the Covenant lies in a tunnel that Solomon constructed directly beneath the Temple he built, looking forward to future invaders. And according to Rabbi Richman, the Temple Institute knows where the Ark is located and will get it when it is needed for building the Third Temple.[42] However, there was an article written in January of 2018 by *Arkfiles.net: Quest for the Truth* entitled "Exposing The Garden Tomb Association," which disputes the claim of the Garden Tomb Association and provides evidence substantiating Wyatt's excavation.[43] In any case, both the Rabbis and Ron Wyatt make good cases for the resting place of the Ark of the Covenant. However, in either case, the Ark of the Covenant is in Jerusalem, very near to the Temple Mount and the construction site of the Third Temple.

After this in Matthew 24:32–34, Jesus concludes with an analogy about the "Fig Tree" budding (speaking of the Nation of Israel becoming a nation again). And, that the generation that sees these events taking place should realize that His return is "very near, right at the door." This further confirms that all these signs discussed above that have been, or are in the process of being, fulfilled since Israel became a nation again in 1948 point to the fact that we are very close to the next event on the eschatological/teleological calendar—the Rapture of the Church! While that concludes the signs of the times discussion, it remains to briefly summarize the entire book before we finally conclude the book and provide recommendations and comments on moving forward.

We began the book by identifying terms that are often identified with Eschatology, or the events surrounding the Second Coming of the Lord Jesus, and laying the biblical, theological, and eschatological/teleological foundation of the Perfect/Complete Gospel and the Parable of the Wheat and the Weeds. Next, we studied the foundational concepts of Biblical Prophecy and its Interpretation, Time and Timelines, and the Kingdom of

Heaven/God. Then after laying this foundation, we studied the Second Coming/Advent of Jesus, or the *Parousia*, in detail. And after that, we then broke down all the related, specific events surrounding the *Parousia* of Jesus:

1) Beliefs about the Millennium;

2) The Old Testament concept of the Day of the LORD (*Yahweh*), or Daniel's Seventieth Week, further defined as of the Tribulation by the New Testament;

3) The beliefs about the Rapture of the Church;

4) Personal Eschatology—related resurrections, judgments, and intermediate and eternal states of humanity; along with

5) The Signs of the Times.

After considering all the information presented by all those chapters, and wrapping all this together into one conclusion for the book, I believe:

1) That we are very close to the end of the Church Age;

2) That the Pretribulational Rapture of the Church (with the associated resurrection of all saints of the historical Body of Christ in the last 2,000 years and the Judgment Seat of Christ and the Marriage Supper of the Lamb occurring in Heaven) is the next event on the teleological calendar, followed by

3) The rise of the Antichrist and the Seven-Year Tribulation Period (with its associated judgments, and raptures of the Midtribulation Saints, the 144,000, and the Two Witnesses), culminating in the Battle of Armageddon, and then,

4) Jesus comes back to earth physically and visibly on the Mount of Olives, destroying the Antichrist, False Prophet, and their entire army (and the Antichrist and False Prophet being thrown into the Lake of Fire). Then, the Old Testament Saints are resurrected and judged first. Next, there will be all the Tribulation Saints who were martyred or were raptured during the Tribulation. And finally, there are the living Jews first, and then, "all the nations" (living Gentiles) who survived the

Tribulation and who will be judged by Jesus. The living believers repopulate the earth in the Millennial Kingdom, and the unbelievers are judged and sent to their Intermediate States, followed by

5) Satan/the devil being bound for one thousand years; during which time, Jesus reigns on the earth in the Millennial/Messianic Kingdom, with resurrected saints judging, ruling, and reigning with Jesus;

6) At the end of the Millennium, Satan is released for a short time, deceives more people to follow him against Jesus again, is defeated, judged, and also thrown into the Lake of Fire; then,

7) The Great White Throne Judgment takes place, when all unbelievers are judged, and finally

8) God creates a "New Heaven and New Earth," and both believers and unbelievers enter into their final/eternal states: New Jerusalem for believers and the Lake of Fire for unbelievers.

So with all this in the very near future, and with the imminent Rapture of the Church even closer, the final sign of the Perfect/Complete Gospel being preached or taught in the whole earth takes on paramount significance.

Although the Gospel appears to have been preached to almost the entire world, the 2015 numbers show that only 2.3 billion people consider themselves to be Christian, out of 7.4 billion (31.1%).[44] But according to 2 Peter 3:9, even though the Day of the Lord is coming (and we are extremely close to its beginning, based on all the above signs), *God's desire is for none to perish, but all to come to repentance.* Also, remember that God did not create hell for humanity, but for Satan and his angels (Matt 25:41). In the twenty-first century, there have been major revivals in China, India, South America (especially Brazil), and Africa (especially South Africa and Nigeria),[45] and even some minor revivals in North America (e.g., the Toronto Blessing)[46] and Europe.[47] But still, there are over 5 billion people who have not accepted the good news of the Perfect/Complete Gospel: that Jesus is the Christ/Messiah, who was miraculously born into this world of the Holy Spirit and the Virgin Mary, lived a sinless life, died as an atonement for the sins of humanity, and was resurrected, ascended back into heaven, and sits at the right hand of the Father (Apostle's Creed). And all this was done to restore relationship and reconcile God with humanity by grace though faith (Eph 2:4–9), if one confesses with one's mouth Jesus is Lord and believes in one's heart that God raised Him from the dead (Rom 10:9–10).

Although this clear, simple message of the Perfect/Complete Gospel of Both Comings of Jesus Christ has not changed in nearly two thousand years, today in the Laodicean Period of the Church Age and in this Postmodern world, it appears to be overcome by Satan's false gospel of deceit, heresy, and false religions (in light of the Parable of the Wheat and Tares/Weeds), and overshadowed by the apocalyptic eschatological aspect of the end of the world. This seems to be confirmed by the vision Oral Roberts received from the Lord in 2004 (mentioned in chap. 1): that neither the Church nor the world knows about or is ready for the *Parousia*.[48] All this has led the Body of Christ to "such a time as this" in the year of our Lord 2019.

With all this being said, there should be an increased sense of urgency to teach and preach the Perfect/Complete Gospel of Both Comings of Jesus Christ. However, this noticeable decline in teaching and preaching of the Gospel appears to have an inverse relationship to the increase of Satan's promulgation of deceptive and heretical lies, doctrines, and cults (the primary ones being the Illuminati, the New Age Movement, and the meteoric resurgence of Radical Islam). Thus, if there ever was "such a time as this"—to be aware of the Signs of the Times and reinstitute the teaching and preaching of the Perfect/Complete Gospel to all nations—it is now, in order to fulfill Matthew

24:14, Mark 13:10, Luke 24:47, and Romans 16:26. And also, today (even as you are reading this), all Christians should pray for a worldwide, Holy Spirit-generated revival. So that we may join with Paul, John, the Early Church, and the entire Universal Church (Body of Christ today) in saying, "Maranatha, come Lord Jesus!"

Notes

Chapter 1

[1]Unless otherwise indicated all Bible references are to the New American Standard Bible (La Habra, CA: The Lockman Foundation, 1973).

[2]Denis W. Vinyard, ed., *"maranatha," The New Testament Greek-English Dictionary*, vol. 14 (Springfield, MO: The Complete Bible Library, 1990), 112–13.

[3]Spiros Zodhiates, ed., *"eschatos," The Complete Word Study Dictionary, New Testament* (Chattanooga, TN: AMG Publishers, 1992), 661–2.

[4]John H. Leith, ed., *Creeds of the Churches*, 3rd ed. (Louisville: Westminster John Knox Press, 1982), 22–25

[5]John Polkinghorne, *The God of Hope and the End of the World* (New Haven, CT and London: Yale University Press, 2002), 100.

[6]Oral Roberts, interview by Benny Hinn on *This is Your Day*, 20 August 2004.

[7]David K. Hebert, "The Need for Teaching the Eschatological Gospel of Both Comings of Jesus Christ in the Twenty-first Century, Especially as We See the Day of His Parousia Approaching" (D.Th. thesis, University of South Africa [UNISA], 2009).

[8]See J. N Darby, *Synopsis of the Books of the Bible*, vol. 3, *Colossians – Revelation*, 2nd ed. (New York: Loizeaux Bros., 1950), 561–3; C. I. Scofield, ed., *The Scofield Reference Bible* (New York and Oxford, U. K.: Oxford Press, 1945), 1332–4; Edmont Hains, *Seven Churches of Revelation* (Winona Lake, IN, n.d.), 11; Gordon Lindsay, *The Book of Revelation Made Easy – The Seven Churches of Prophecy* (Dallas: The Voice of Healing Publishing, 1961), 17–8; Albert Edmund Johnson, *God's Unveiling of the Future: A Chronological Approach to the Book of Revelation for Laymen, Bible Students, and Ministers* (1978), 15–6; Steve Gregg , ed., *Revelation: Four Views, A Parallel*

Commentary (Nashville: Thomas Nelson, 1997), 62–3 for details on Seven Church Periods of the Church Age.

[9]Michael Blanchard, "Be Ye Glad," http://www.noelpaulstookey.com/06-14.html/ (18 June 2019), 1980 Newspring Publishing Inc. (ASCAP) (adm. at Capitol CMG Publishing,.com/GotzMusic). Used by permission.

[10]Establishment of Israel: The Declaration of the Establishment of the State of Israel (May 14, 1948), 6 January 2013, http://www.jewishvirtuallibrary.org/jsource/History/Dec_of_Indep.html/ (18 June 2013).

[11]*The World Book Encyclopedia (Chicago: World Book, 2001)*, 1:31; 3:29; *The Timechart of Biblical History* (*Chippenham, England: Third Millennium Press, 2002*), I; John J. Butt, *The Greenwood Dictionary of World History* (Westport, CT: Greenwood, 2006), 19; Michael Rood, "Biblical Hebrew Calendar," http://www.michaelrood.com/hebrew_calendar.htm/ (20 March 2007).

[12]William J. Dumbrell, *The Search for Order: Biblical Eschatology in Focus* (Grand Rapids: Baker, 1994), 15–95; William Sanford LaSor, David Allan Hubbard, and Frederic Wm. Bush, *Old Testament Survey: The Message, Form, and Background of the Old Testament*, 2nd ed. (Grand Rapids: Eerdmans, 1996), 4.

[13]Dumbrell, 57–152.

[14]Dumbrell, 153–258.

[15]James 5:3; 7–9; Romans 8:18–24; 1 Corinthians 15; Ephesians 1:3–14; 1 Thessalonians 1:3, 9–10; 3:13; 4:13–18; 5:8–11; Titus 2:11–13; 1 Peter 1:3–12; 2:4–10; 4:1–7; 2 Peter 1:11, 16, 19; 3; Hebrews 9:12–28; 10:37–12:2, 26–7; Jude 14–23; 1 John 2:14–3:3; and Revelation.

[16]Dumbrell, 259–346.

[17]Herschel H. Hobbs, "The Gospel of the Blessed Hope," *Christianity Today* 2 (Dec. 23, 1957):13.

[18]Zodhiates, *"eschatos,"* 661–2.

[19]Gerhard Kittel and Gerhard Friedrich, eds., *"telos ";* *"teleios";* *Theological Dictionary of the New Testament, Abridged in One Vol.*,

trans. Geoffrey W. Bromiley (Grand Rapids: Eerdmans, 1985), 1161, 1164–5.

[20]Zodhiates, *"euangelion,"* 669.

[21]Verlyn D. Verbrugge, ed. *"martyreo/martyria," The NIV Theological Dictionary of New Testament Words* (Grand Rapids: Zondervan, 2000), 485.

[22]David W. Dorries, *Our Christian Roots*, vol.1 (Coweta, OK: Kairos Ministries International, 2002), 13.

[23]Larry D. Hart, *Truth Aflame: A Balanced Theology for Evangelicals and Charismatics* (Nashville: Thomas Nelson, 1999), 13–15.

[24]Dorries, 12; Bengt Hagglund, *History of Theology*, trans. Gene J. Lund (St. Louis: Concordia Publishing, 1968), 45, 50, 53, 65, 79.

[25]H. E. W. Turner, *The Pattern of Christian Truth: A Study in the Relations between Orthodoxy and Heresy in the Early Church* (London: A. R. Mowbray, 1954; reprint, New York: AMS Press, 1978), 3–6.

[26]Dorries, 13.

[27]Turner, 475–9.

[28]Alan W. Gomes, *Unmasking the Cults* (Grand Rapids: Zondervan, 1995), 10–11.

[29]Zodhiates, *"orthos,"* 52, 941, 1127.

[30]Kittel and Friedrich, *"dokeo,"* 178.

[31]Mircea Eliade, ed., "orthodoxy," *The Encyclopedia of Religion*, vol. 11 (New York: Macmillan, 1987), 124.

[32]Eliade, vol. 6, "heresy," 269–70.

[33]Robin Keeley, ed., *Eerdmans Handbook to Christian Belief* (Grand Rapids: Eerdmans, 1982), 468.

Chapter 2

[1]Norman L. Geisler, *Systematic Theology: In One Volume* (Minneapolis: Bethany House, 2011), 169–70.

[2]Geisler, *One Volume*, 174.

[3]Geisler, *One Volume*, 178.

[4]Geisler, *One Volume*, 369.

[5]Geisler, *One Volume*, 370–71.

[6]David W. Dorries, *Our Christian Roots*, vol.1 (Coweta, OK: Kairos Ministries International, 2002), 13.

[7]Dorries, 13.

[8]Geisler, *One Volume*, 383–4 (See page 384 for complete list of these books).

[9]Gordon D. Fee and Douglas Stuart, *How to Read the Bible for All Its Worth*, 4th ed. (Grand Rapids, MI: Zondervan, 2014), 27–28.

[10]Norman Geisler, *Systematic Theology*, vol. 4, *Church/Last Things* (Minneapolis: Bethany House, 2005), 415–17, 451.

[11]William W. Klein, Craig L. Blomberg, and Robert L. Hubbard, Jr., *Introduction to Biblical Interpretation* (Nashville: Thomas Nelson, 1993), 359, 370–78; William Sanford LaSor, David Allan Hubbard and Frederic Wm. Bush, *Old Testament Survey: The Message, Form, and Background of the Old Testament*, 2nd ed. (Grand Rapids: Eerdmans, 1996), 229–30.

[12]Robert H. Stein, *A Basic Guide to Interpreting the Bible: Playing by the Rules* (Grand Rapids: Baker, 2004), 89; Klein, Blomberg, and Robert Hubbard, 384–5; LaSor, David Hubbard, and Bush, 569–70.

[13]Fee and Stuart, 260.

[14]Klein, Blomberg, and Robert Hubbard, 375–7.

[15]J. Dwight Pentecost, *Things to Come: A Study in Biblical Eschatology* (Findlay, OH: Dunham Publishing; reprint, Grand Rapids: Zondervan, 1981), 50–59.

[16]Pentecost, 60–64.

[17]Fee and Stuart, 44–45.

[18]Nancy Jean Vyhmeister and Terry Dwain Robertson, *Quality Research Papers: For Students of Religion and Theology* (Grand Rapids, MI: Zondervan, 2014), chap. 2.

[19]John F. Walvoord, *Revelation*, ed. Philip E. Rawley and Mark Hitchcock (Chicago: Moody, 2011), 21–23.

[20]Kenneth L. Gentry Jr., "A Preterist View of Revelation," in *Four Views on the Book of Revelation*, ed. C. Marvin Pate (Grand Rapids, MI: Zondervan, 1998), 37.

[21]C. Marvin Pate, ed., *Four Views on the Book of Revelation* (Grand Rapids, MI: Zondervan, 1998), 19–22.

[22]Walvoord, 22.

[23]Pate, 20.

[24]Pate, 23.

[25]Walvoord, 21; Pate, 24.

[26]Pentecost, 16–20.

[27]Walvoord, 23.

[28]Le Roy Edwin Froom, *The Prophetic Faith of our Fathers, The Historical Development of Prophetic Interpretation*, vol. 1, *Early Church Exposition, Subsequent Deflections, and Medieval Revival* (Washington, DC: Review and Herald, 1950), 683, 692–696; Richard Kyle, *The Last Days are Here Again: A History of the End Times* (Grand Rapids, MI: Baker, 1998), 47–49.

[29]Walvoord, 23.

[30]Pate, 30.

[31]Walvoord, 24.

Chapter 3

[1]Markus Pössel, "The Case of the Travelling Twins," *Einstein Online* 4 (2010), 1007.

[2]Willem A. Van Gemeren, ed., *"et," New International Dictionary of Old Testament Theology and Exegesis* (*NIDOTTE*), vol. 3 (Grand Rapids, MI: Zondervan, 1997), 564–6.

[3]Van Gemeren, *"yom," NIDOTTE*, vol. 2, 419–23.

[4]Spiros Zodhiates, ed., *"chronos," The Complete Word Study Dictionary, New Testament* (Chattanooga, TN: AMG Publishers, 1992), 1487.

[5]Zodhiates, *"kairos,"* 805.

[6]Walther Eichrodt, *Theology of the Old Testament,* vol. 1, trans. J. A. Baker (Philadelphia: Westminster Press, 1961); Walther Eichrodt, *Theology of the Old Testament,* vol. 2, trans. J. A. Baker (Philadelphia: Westminster Press, 1967).

[7]Richard Bauckham, and Trevor Hart, "The Shape of Time," in *The Future as God's Gift: Explorations in Christian Eschatology,* ed. David Fergusson and Marcel Sarot (Edinburgh: T & T Clark, 2000), 72.

[8]Luco J. Van den Brom, "Eschatology and Time: Reversal of the Time Direction?" in *The Future as God's Gift: Explorations in Christian Eschatology,* ed. David Fergusson and Marcel Sarot (Edinburgh: T & T Clark, 2000), 167.

[9]Christoph Schwöbel, "Last Things First?," in *The Future as God's Gift: Explorations in Christian Eschatology,* ed. David Fergusson and Marcel Sarot (Edinburgh: T & T Clark, 2000), 240–1.

[10]Howard M. Ervin, *Conversion-Initiation and the Baptism in the Holy Spirit: A Critique of James D. G. Dunn, Baptism in the Holy Spirit* (Peabody, MA: Hendrickson, 1984), 2–3.

[11]Victor P. Hamilton, *The Book of Genesis, Chapters 1–17,* The New International Commentary of the Old Testament (Grand Rapids: Eerdmans, 1990), 199.

[12]C. F. Keil and F. Delitzsch, *The Pentateuch,* Biblical Commentary

on the Old Testament, vol. 1, trans. James Martin (Grand Rapids: Eerdmans, 1949),102; Michael Esses, *Jesus in Genesis* (Plainfield, NJ: Logos International, 1974), 19–20; Charles C. Ryrie, *The Ryrie Study Bible* (Chicago: Moody Press, 1978), 12; Kenneth O. Gangel and Stephen J. Bramer, *Genesis*, Holman Old Testament Commentary (Nashville: Broadman and Holman, 2002), 44.

[13]Ervin, *Conversion-Initiation*, 1–3.

[14]Howard M. Ervin, *Spirit Baptism: A Biblical Investigation* (Peabody, MA: Hendrickson, 2002), 5.

[15]Oral Roberts, *Christ in Every Book* (Tulsa: Oral Roberts Evangelistic Association, 1975).

[16]Walter A. Elwell and Robert W. Yarbrough, *Encountering the New Testament: A Historical and Theological Survey* (Grand Rapids: Baker, 1998), 71; H. Wayne House, *Chronological and Background Charts of the New Testament* (Grand Rapids: Zondervan, 1981), 98–100.

[17]Alan Hugh West, "An Exegesis of Revelation 11:15," *Faith and Mission* 16, no. 3 (Summer 1999): 14–21. See also: William E. Biederwolf, *The Second Coming Bible Commentary* (Grand Rapids: Baker, 1924; reprint, 1985); J. Christiaan Beker, *Paul's Apocalyptic Gospel: The Coming Triumph of God* (Philadelphia: Fortress Press, 1982); and Marvin R. Vincent, *Word Studies in the New Testament*, vols. 1–4 (Grand Rapids: Eerdmans, 1946; reprint, Peabody, MA: Hendrickson, 1991).

[18]John J. Butt, *The Greenwood Dictionary of World History* (Westport, CT: Greenwood Press, 2006), 19; *The World Book Encyclopedia* (Chicago: World Book, 2001), vol. 1, 31; vol. 3, 29; Michael J. Radwin, *Hebrew Date Converter*, 2007, http://www.hebcal.com/converter (10 April 2007).

[19]Michael Rood, *Biblical Hebrew Calendar*, 2007, http://www.michaelrood.com/hebrew_calendar.htm/ (20 March 2007).

[20]William J. Dumbrell, *The Search for Order: Biblical Eschatology in Focus* (Grand Rapids: Baker, 1994), 15–23.

[21]See the following: *The Apostolic Fathers, The Letter of Barnabas* 15, trans. Francis X. Glimm, Joseph M. F. Marique, and Gerald

G. Walsh (Washington, DC: The Catholic University of America Press, 1962), 4–5; Thomas B. Falls, *The Writings of Saint Justin Martyr, Dialogue with Trypho* 81 (Washington, DC: The Catholic University of America Press, 1948; reprint, 1965); Julius Africanus, *The Extant Writings of Julius Africanus* 3:18:4, in vol. 6 of *The Ante Nicene Fathers* (*ANF*), ed. Alexander Roberts and James Donaldson (1886; reprint, Peabody, MA: Hendrickson, 1995); Commodianus, *Instructions of Commodianus* 35, in vol. 4 of the *ANF*, ed. Alexander Roberts and James Donaldson (1885; reprint, Peabody, MA: Hendrickson, 1995); Hippolytus; quoted in George Eldon Ladd, *The Blessed Hope* (Grand Rapids: Eerdmans, 1956), 30–1; Lactantius, *The Divine Institutes*, in vol. 7 of *ANF*, ed. Alexander Roberts and James Donaldson (1886; reprint, Peabody, MA: Hendrickson, 1995), 14, 25.

[22]For more information on the "Five-Tiered Model," see Walter Albert Rogero II, "Increasing Knowledge of Christian Cosmogonic Presuppositions," (D. Min. proj., Oral Roberts University, 2015).

[23]See Henry M. Morris, *Scientific Creationism*, 2nd ed. (El Cajon, CA: Creation-Life, 1985); *Biblical Creationism: What Each Book of the Bible Teaches about Creation and the Flood* (Grand Rapids, MI: Baker, 1994); and Henry Morris, ed., *The Henry Morris Study Bible*, rep. ed. (Green Forest, AR: New Leaf, 2012) for more information.

[24]See Hugh Ross, *The Creator and the Cosmos: How the Greatest Scientific Discoveries of the Century Reveal God* (Colorado Springs: NavPress, 1993) and *Creation and Time* (Colorado Springs: NavPress, 1994) for more information.

[25]See Francis S. Collins, *The Language of God: A Scientist Presents Evidence for Belief* (New York: Free Press, 2006) and Denis O. Lamoureux, *Evolutionary Creation: A Christian Approach to Evolution* (Cambridge, England: The Lutterworth Press, 2008) for more information

[26]See Ian G. Barbour, *Religion and Science: Historical and Contemporary Issues* (San Francisco: HarperSanFrancisco, 1997) for more information.

[27]See Edward B. Davis and Robin Collins, "Scientific Naturalism," in *Science and Religion: A Historical Introduction*, ed. Gary B. Frengren (Baltimore: The Johns Hopkins University Press, 2002), 322–334; John H. Haught, "Science and Scientism," *Zygon* 40, no. 2 (June 2005): 363–368; and Tina Beattie, *The New Atheists: The*

Twilight of Reason and the War on Religion (Maryknoll, NY: Orbis, 2008) for more information.

[28]Colin H. Deal, *The Day and Hour Jesus will Return* (P.O. Box 455, Rutherford College, NC: Colin H. Deal, 1981); Ann Spangler and Lois Tverberg, *Sitting at the Feet of Rabbi Jesus* (Grand Rapids: Zondervan, 2009), 104–110, 114–124.

[29]Deal 1981, *The Day and Hour*, 124–141.

[30]Deal 1981, *The Day and Hour*, 142–153; Biederwolf, 12; See also, Ann Spangler, and Lois Tverberg, *Sitting at the Feet of Rabbi Jesus* (Grand Rapids: Zondervan, 2009).

[31]Ryrie, 1327; Norman Geisler, *Systematic Theology*, vol. 4, *Church/ Last Things* (Minneapolis: Bethany House, 2005), 472; Biederwolf, 218.

[32]Jay P. Green Sr., ed. and trans., *The Interlinear Bible; Hebrew-Greek-English.* 2nd ed. (Peabody, MA: Hendrickson, 1986), 691.

[33]Butt, 19; *World Book* 2001, 1:31; 3:29; Robert Wilde, "A.D," *About European History*, 2007, http://european history.about.com/od/ referenceencyclopedia/g/glad/ (10 April 2007); Ernest L. Martin, *The Birth of Christ Recalculated*, 2nd ed. (Pasadena, CA: Foundation for Biblical Research, 1980), 1–2, 132–152.

[34]H. Wayne House, *Chronological and Background Charts of the New Testament* (Grand Rapids: Zondervan, 1981), 64.

[35]Frederick A. Larson, Executive Producer and Presenter, *The Star of Bethlehem Documentary* (Mpower Pictures, 2007); see also, http://www.bethlehemstar.net/

[36]"The Romans Destroy the Temple at Jerusalem, 70 AD," *EyeWitness to History*, 2005, http://www.eyewitnesstohistory.com/ (19 June 2015).

[37]Ryrie, 1327; Biederwolf, 223–5; Geisler, Vol. 4, 597–600.

[38]Charles Herbermann and Georg Grupp, "Constantine the Great," *The Catholic Encyclopedia*, vol. 4 (New York: Robert Appleton Company, 1908): n.p., http://www.newadvent.org/cathen/04295c.htm/ (19 June 2015).

[39]George T. Dennis, "1054 The East-West Schism," *Christianity Today* 28 (1990): n.p., http://www.christianitytoday.com/ch/1990/issue28/2820.html/ (19 June 2015).

[40]Biederwolf, 202–4, 208; Richard Kyle, *The Last Days Are Here Again: A History of the End Times* (Grand Rapids: Baker, 1998), 126–129.

[41]Colin H. Deal, *The Beast and the Arabs* (P. O. Box 455, Rutherford College, NC: Colin H. Deal, 1983); Colin H. Deal, *Revelation of the Beast* (P. O. Box 455, Rutherford College, NC: Colin H. Deal, 1995), 9–74; J. R. Church, *Hidden Prophecies in the Psalms* (Oklahoma City: Prophecy Publications, 1986), 225–6.

[42]"Roman Empire," 2006, http://www.roman-empire.net/ (30 September 2006).

[43]"Arab League," 2015, http://en.wikipedia.org/wiki/Arab_League/ (18 May 2015).

[44]"The Death of Alexander the Great, 323 BC," *EyeWitness to History*, 2008, http://www.eyewitnesstohistory.com/ (19 May 2015).

[45]"Alexander's Four Generals," *Like the Master Ministries*, 2006, http://www.neverthirsty.org/pp/series/DAN/D013/D0134.html/ (18 May 2015).

[46]Rick Lanser, "Understanding the 2,300 'Evenings and Mornings' of Daniel 8:14," *Associates for Biblical Research*, 30 April 2018, n.p., http://www.biblearchaeology.org/post/2018/04/30/Understanding-the-2300-e2809cEvenings-and-Morningse2809d-of-Daniel-814.aspx#Article/ (18 September 2018); Fred P. Miller, "The 2300 Day Prophecy of Daniel 8," Moellerhaus Publishers, 1999–2016, n.p., http://www.moellerhaus.com/2300.htm/ (18 September 2018).

Chapter 4

[1]Howard M. Ervin, *Conversion-Initiation and the Baptism in the Holy Spirit: A Critique of James D. G. Dunn, Baptism in the Holy Spirit* (Peabody, MA: Hendrickson, 1984), 2–3.

[2]Willem A.Van Gemeren, ed. *"malkut," New International Dictionary of Old Testament Theology and Exegesis*, vol. 2 (Grand Rapids: Zondervan, 1997), 956–63; *"shamayim,"* vol. 4,160–6.

[3]Spiros Zodhiates, ed., *"basileia," The Complete Word Study Dictionary, New Testament* (Chattanooga, TN: AMG Publishers, 1992), 325–7.

[4]Michael Lattke, "On the Jewish Background of the Synoptic Concept: The Kingdom of God," in *The Kingdom of God in the Teaching of Jesus,* vol. 5 in the Issues in Religion and Theology Series, ed. Bruce Chilton (Philadelphia: Fortress Press, 1984), 72–3.

[5]William V. McDonald, "Chapter 3: The Kingdom of Heaven in its Historical Setting," in *A Hebrew Text in Greek Dress: A Comparison and Contrast between Jewish and Hellenistic Thought,* 2nd ed. (Austin, TX: New Life Teaching Center, New Life Ministries, 2014).

[6]George Eldon Ladd, *Theology of the New Testament* (Grand Rapids: Eerdmans, 1974), 45–6.

[7]William W. Klein, Craig L. Blomberg, and Robert L. Hubbard Jr., *Introduction to Biblical Interpretation* (Nashville: Thomas Nelson, 1993), 375–7.

[8]Arthur Green, *These are the Words: A Vocabulary of Jewish Spiritual Life* (Woodstock, VT: Jewish Light Publishing, 1999), 23–4.

[9]See Gerhard von Rad, *Theological Dictionary of the New Testament,* vol. 1, 567–69. Also, John Bright's excellent books deal almost exclusively with the Kingdom of God as a future hope.

[10]Ladd, *Theology of the New Testament,* 61.

[11]Charles C. Ryrie, *The Ryrie Study Bible* (Chicago: Moody Press, 1978), 1305; William Sanford LaSor, David Allan Hubbard, and Frederic Wm. Bush, *Old Testament Survey: The Message, Form, and Background of the Old Testament,* 2nd ed. (Grand Rapids: Eerdmans, 1996), 574.

[12]William J. Dumbrell, *The Search for Order: Biblical Eschatology in Focus* (Grand Rapids: Baker, 1994.), 131–3; Ladd, *Theology of the New Testament,* 61; Lattke, 78–82.

[13]Norman Geisler, *Systematic Theology,* vol. 4, *Church/Last Things* (Minneapolis: Bethany House, 2005), 459.

[14]Geisler, Vol. 4, 497.

[15]Geisler, Vol. 4, 465–470.

[16]Thurman Wisdom, "The Valley of Decision (Joel 3)," *Biblical Viewpoint* 29 (1995): 35.

[17]Dumbrell, 136; Geisler, Vol. 4, 470–2; LaSor, David Hubbard, and Bush, 566.

[18]Psalms 2:1–12; 8:4–8; 22:28–31; 24:7–10; Isaiah 2:1–5; 4:2–6; 9:7; 11:4–12; 32; 35:1–10; 56:6–7; 60; 66:7–9; Daniel 2:44; Hosea 6:2; Joel 2:28–32; Obadiah 17–21; Micah 5:1–15; see William E. Biederwolf, *The Second Coming Bible Commentary* (Grand Rapids: Baker, 1924; reprint, 1985), 28–30, 30–2, 46, 51–2, 55–7, 58–62, 91–3, 100–02, 109, 112–17, 136–140, 201, 204, 245, 251–2, 261–2, 266–8; Psalms 95–106; see J. R. Church, *Hidden Prophecies in the Psalms* (Oklahoma City: Prophecy Publications, 1986), 47, 282–301.

[19]Biederwolf, 32–4, 37–9, and 254–6.

[20]Church, 191, 216, 318, and 362–3.

[21]Jeremiah 3:14–18; 23:1–8; 29:12–14; 30:1–3; 32:36–44; 50:4–7, 19–20, 33–34; Ezekiel 11:17–21; 28:25–6; 29:21; 34:11–31; 36 – 37; Hosea 1:10–11; 3:5; 12:9; 13:14; Amos 9:11–15; Micah 2:12–3; 4:1–13; 7:1–20; Zephaniah 3:11–20; Haggai 2:6–9; and Zechariah 8; see Biederwolf 146–48, 149–155, 165–66, 170–72, 180–84, 242–3, 245–6, 259–60; 263–266, 269–70, 273–8, and 292–4; and Psalms 48:4–7, 11–13; 51:7; 67; 69:35–6; 73; 84:1–2, 4, 10; and 85:1, 6, 9, 13, see Church, 150–2, 157–8, 183, 201–4, 227– 36.

[22]Brad H. Young, *The Parables: Jewish Tradition and Christian Interpretation* (Peabody, MA: Hendrickson, 1998), 146, 199–202, 207–8, 220–1.

[23]This is further amplified by the collection of essays written in *The Kingdom of God in the Teaching of Jesus*, edited by Bruce Chilton (1984); and the sections on "The Kingdom of God" in Ladd's, *A Theology of the New Testament* (1974); and Geisler's, *Systematic Theology*, vol. 4, *Church/Last Things* (2005).

[24]Dumbrell, 127, 152; Richard Kyle, *The Last Days Are Here Again: A History of the End Times* (Grand Rapids: Baker, 1998), 28–30.

[25]See Menahem Mansoor, *The Dead Sea Scrolls: A Textbook and Study Guide*, 2nd ed. (Grand Rapids: Baker, 1983), 153–162; Lattke,

72–3; Alfred Edersheim, *The Life and Times of Jesus the Messiah* (Peabody, MA: Hendrickson, 1993), 26–7, 925–928; Kyle, 31; Dale C. Allison, Jr., "The Eschatology of Jesus," in *The Continuum History of Apocalypticism*, ed. Bernard McGinn, John J. Collins, and Stephen J. Stein (New York, London: Continuum, 2003), 145, 147–8; John J. Collins, "From Prophecy to Apocalypticism: The Expectation of the End," in *The Continuum History of Apocalypticism*, ed. Bernard McGinn, John J. Collins, and Stephen J. Stein (New York, London: Continuum, 2003), 64–80; Florentino Garcia Martinez, "Apocalypticism in the Dead Sea Scrolls," in *The Continuum History of Apocalypticism*, ed. Bernard McGinn, John J. Collins, and Stephen J. Stein, (New York, London: Continuum, 2003), 89–92, 96, 101, 105, 110; and James C. VanderKam, "Messianism and Apocalypticism," in *The Continuum History of Apocalypticism*, ed. Bernard McGinn, John J. Collins, and Stephen J. Stein (New York, London: Continuum, 2003), 112–115, 134–137.

[26]Allison Jr., 146.

[27]Hans Bald, "Eschatological or Theocentric Ethics?" in *The Kingdom of God in the Teaching of Jesus*, vol. 5, in the Issues in Religion and Theology Series, ed. Bruce Chilton (Philadelphia: Fortress Press, 1984), 133; Chilton, 1–3; Erich Grasser, "On Understanding the Kingdom of God," in *The Kingdom of God in the Teaching of Jesus*, vol. 5, in the Issues in Religion and Theology Series, ed. Bruce Chilton (Philadelphia: Fortress Press, 1984), 52–3, 64; Werner Georg Kummel, "Eschatological Expectation in the Proclamation of Jesus," in *The Kingdom of God in the Teaching of Jesus*, vol. 5, in the Issues in Religion and Theology Series, ed. Bruce Chilton (Philadelphia: Fortress Press, 1984), 36–7; Ladd, 45–8, 57.

[28]Joachim Jeremias, *The Parables of Jesus*, 2nd rev. ed. (Upper Saddle River, NJ: Prentice-Hall, 1972), 230, 247–8; Chilton, 1–3; Ladd, *Theology of the New Testament*, 91, 93–104; Marvin R. Vincent, *Word Studies in the New Testament*, vol. 1 (Grand Rapids: Eerdmans, 1946; reprint, Peabody, MA: Hendrickson, 1991), 311; Geisler, Vol. 4, 477–485.

[29]Young, 37, 275.

[30]See W. H. Robinson, *The Parables of Jesus in Their Relation to His Ministry* (Chicago: University of Chicago Press, 1928); A. T. Cadoux, *The Parables of Jesus: Their Art and Use* (London: J. Clarke, 1930); C. H. Dodd, *The Parables of the Kingdom* (New York: Charles Scribner's Sons, 1936), 32; Robert H. Stein, *An Introduction*

to the Parables of Jesus (Philadelphia: The Westminster Press, 1981), 58–9.

[31]Young, 278–9.

[32]Ladd, *Theology of the New Testament*, 94–103; Biederwolf, 319; Geisler, Vol. 4, 483, 485.

[33]Young, 82.

[34]Alva J. McClain, *The Greatness of the Kingdom* (Winona Lake, IN: BHM, 1974), 343–3; Geisler, Vol. 4, 483–4.

[35]Young, 119.

[36]Young, 69–70.

[37]Young, 171–2, 186.

[38]Young, 282–3.

[39]J. Dwight Pentecost, *The Parables of Jesus* (Grand Rapids: Baker, Zondervan, 1982), 149–155.

[40]See George A. Buttrick, *The Parables of Jesus* (New York: Harper and Row, 1928), 253–6; Herbert Lockyer, *All the Parables of the Bible* (Grand Rapids: Zondervan, 1963), 246; Jeremias, 206–10; Simon J. Kistemaker, *The Parables of Jesus* (Grand Rapids: Baker, 1980), 146; Stein, 131; Pentecost, *The Parables of Jesus*, 157; A. M. Hunter, *The Parables for Today* (London: SCM Press, 1983), 75; David Wenham, *The Parables of Jesus* (Downers Grove, IL: InterVarsity Press, 1989), 88–9; Young, 295; and Arland J. Hulgren, *The Parables of Jesus, A Commentary* (Grand Rapids: Eerdmans, 2000), 310.

[41]David K. Hebert, "A Course Synthesis Paper on The Parable of the Sheep and the Goats (Matthew 25:31–46)," a paper presented for GBIB 583, The Parables of Jesus in their Jewish Context, ORU, 2005.

[42]For more information on this conclusion, see Lockyer, 246–7; Stein, 130–40; and Pentecost, *The Parables of Jesus*, 149–55.

[43]Chilton, 1–2.

[44]Biederwolf, 322–4, 371–5.

[45]Vincent, vol. 1, 352–3.

[46]Biederwolf, 314–5, 368–9.

[47]This breakdown of the Periods of the Church Age is a compilation of the following theologians on the matter: J. N. Darby, *Synopsis of the Books of the Bible*, vol. 3, Colossians – Revelation, 2nd ed. (New York: Loizeaux Brothers, 1950), 561–3; C. I. Scofield, ed., *The Scofield Reference Bible* (New York and Oxford: Oxford Press, 1945), 1332–4; Edmont Hains, *Seven Churches of Revelation* (Winona Lake, IN, n.d.), 11; Gordon Lindsay, *The Book of Revelation Made Easy – The Seven Churches of Prophecy* (Dallas: The Voice of Healing Publishing, 1961), 17–8; Albert Edmund Johnson, *God's Unveiling of the Future: A Chronological Approach to the Book of Revelation for Laymen, Bible Students and Ministers* (1978), 15–6; and Steve Gregg, ed., *Revelation: Four Views, A Parallel Commentary* (Nashville: Thomas Nelson, 1997), 62–3.

[48]Bill T. Arnold and Bryan Beyer, *Encountering the Old Testament: A Christian Survey*, Encountering Biblical Studies Series (Grand Rapids: Baker, 1999), 36–40, 45; Sandra L. Richter, *The Epic of Eden: A Christian Entry Into the Old Testament* (Downers Grove, IL: InterVarsity Press, 2008), 55–56.

[49]George E. Mendenhall, *Ancient Israel's Faith and History: An Introduction to the Bible in Context*, ed. Gary A. Herion (Louisville: Westminster John Knox Press, 2001), 30.

[50]Alan J. Avery-Peck, "covenant," *The Encyclopedia of Judaism*, vol. 1, ed. Jacob Neusner, et al. (New York: Continuum, 1999), 137–138.

[51]Richter, 74–75.

[52]Fred Skolnik, Shmuel Himelstein, and Geoffrey Wigoder, eds., "covenant," *The New Encyclopedia of Judaism* (New York: NYU Press, 2002), 187; Richter, 77.

[53]Skolnik, Himelstein, and Wigoder, "covenant," 187.

[54]Dennis J. McCarthy, *Treaty and Covenant: A Study in Form in the Ancient Oriental Documents and in the Old Testament* (Rome: Pontifical Biblical Institute, 1963), 55.

[55]Avery-Peck, 137.

[56]Eugene F. Roop, "Two Become One Become Two," *Brethren Life and Thought* 21, no. 3 (June 1, 1976): 134–135, *ATLA Religion Database*, EBSCOhost (11 October 2014); Isabelle V. De Lima Sylvester, "Divine Covenantal Love: The Basis of the Abrahamic Covenant," (M.A. thesis, Oral Roberts University, 2014), 21.

[57]Norman Geisler, *Systematic Theology in One Volume* (Minneapolis: Bethany House, 2011), 1379–1386; J. Dwight Pentecost, *Things to Come: A Study in Biblical Eschatology* (Grand Rapids: Zondervan, 1964), 70–73, 93–4.

[58]Geisler, *One Volume*, 1386–1391.

[59]Pentecost, *Things to Come*, 95–99.

[60]Geisler, *One Volume*, 1391–92.

[61]Pentecost, *Things to Come*, 116–119; Geisler, *One Volume*, 1392–1396.

[62]Charles C. Ryrie, *Dispensationalism* (Chicago: Moody Press, 1995), 65–67.

[63]Walter A. Elwell, "Dispensationalism," *Evangelical Dictionary of Theology*, rev. ed. (Grand Rapids: Baker, 2001), 343–5.

[64]Richard Kyle, *The Last Days Are Here Again: A History of the End Times* (Grand Rapids: Baker, 1998), 117; Darrell L. Bock, "Charting Dispensationalism," *Christianity Today* (12 September 1994): 26–29. Also, see Ryrie's *Dispensationalism* (1995) for more specific details on Dispensationalism.

[65]Ryrie, *Dispensationalism*, 183–187.

[66]Matt Slick, "What is Replacement Theology?" *Christian Apologetics & Research Ministry (CARM)*, n.p., https://carm.org/questions-replacement-theology/ (24 May 2016).

[67]Francis Brown, Edward Robinson, S. R. Driver, and Charles A. Briggs, "chesed," *The New Brown, Driver, Briggs, Gesenius Hebrew and English Lexicon: With an Appendix Containing the Biblical Aramaic* (Peabody, MA: Hendrickson, 1979), 338–339.

Chapter 5

[1]Walter A. Elwell and Robert W. Yarbrough, *Encountering the New Testament: A Historical and Theological Survey* (Grand Rapids: Baker, 1998), 71; H. Wayne House, *Chronological and Background Charts of the New Testament* (Grand Rapids: Zondervan, 1981), 98–100.

[2]Lee Strobel, *The Case for Christ* (Grand Rapids: Zondervan, 1998), 77–84.

[3]Spiros Zodhiates, ed., "*erchomai*," *The Complete Word Study Dictionary, New Testament* (Chattanooga, TN: AMG Publishers, 1992), 656–8.

[4]*The Online Greek Bible,* "*erchomenon*," 2004, n.p., *http://greekbible.com/* (31 October 2005).

[5]Zodhiates, "*parousia*," 1123–4.

[6]Denis W. Vinyard, ed., "*maranatha*," *The New Testament Greek-English Dictionary*, vol. 14 (Springfield, MO: The Complete Bible Library, 1990), 112–13; Marvin R. Vincent, "*maranatha*," *Word Studies in the New Testament*, vol. 3 (Grand Rapids: Eerdmans, 1946; reprint, Peabody, MA: Hendrickson, 1991), 289.

[7]Zodhiates, "*maranatha*," 943.

[8]Charles C. Ryrie, *The Ryrie Study Bible* (Chicago: Moody Press, 1978), 1751.

[9]I. N. Johns, *The Reference Passage Bible New Testament, with Old Testament References* (Plainfield, NJ: Logos International, 1978), 960–1, 1400–1, 1326–8, 628–9.

[10]Thomas B. Falls, *The Writings of Saint Justin Martyr, Dialogue with Trypho* (Washington, DC: The Catholic University of America Press, 1948; reprint, 1965), 220–330.

[11]William E. Biederwolf, *The Second Coming Bible Commentary* (Grand Rapids: Baker, 1924; reprint, 1985), 10.

[12]Biederwolf, 32–33.

[13]Biederwolf, 39–40.

[14]Biederwolf, 41–43.

[15]Biederwolf, 55–57.

[16]Biederwolf, 118–121.

[17]Biederwolf, 140–146.

[18]Biederwolf, 201, 204–5.

[19]Biederwolf, 205, 210.

[20]Biederwolf, 266–268.

[21]Biederwolf, 304–308.

[22]Biederwolf, 309–313.

[23]J. R. Church, *Hidden Prophecies in the Psalms* (Oklahoma City: Prophecy Publications, 1986), 46–48.

[24]Church, 91.

[25]Church, 152.

[26]Church, 225–227.

[27]Church, 234–236.

[28]Church, 246.

[29]Church, 281.

[30]Church, 314.

[31]Church, 360.

[32]James W. Watts, "Psalm 2 in the Context of Biblical Theology," *Horizons in Biblical Theology* 12, no. 1 (1990): 73–91.

[33]Merling Alomia, "The Psalm of the 'Blessed Hope': Comments on Psalm 126," in *To Understand the Scriptures: Essays in Honor of William H. Shea* (Berrien Springs, MI: Institute of Archaeology;

Siegfried H. Horn Archaeological Museum Andrews University, 1997), 45–56.

[34]Alan Hugh West, "An Exegesis of Revelation 11:15," *Faith and Mission* 16, no. 3 (Summer 1999): 14.

[35]Brent Kinman, "Parousia, Jesus' 'Triumphal' Entry, and the Fate of Jerusalem," *Journal of Biblical Literature* 118 (Summer 1999): 288–90, 293–4.

[36]Elwell and Yarbrough, 78–85.

[37]Papias, *Fragments of Papias* 6 (*ANF* 1:154–5); Eusebius, *The Church History of Eusebius* 3.24.6, n. 5, (*NPNF* 1:152–3, 3.39.16); *NPNF* 1:173.

[38]*The New Testament in Hebrew and English* (Edgware, Middlesex, UK: The Society of Distributing the Holy Scriptures to the Jews, 1981), 52–55.

[39]William Wilson, *Old Testament Word Studies* (Grand Rapids: Kregel Publications, 1978), 82–6; George V. Wigram, *The New Englishman's Hebrew Concordance* (Peabody, MA: Hendrickson, 1984), 182–3.

[40]Lancelot C. L. Brenton, *The Septuagint with Apocrypha: Greek and English* (London: Samuel Bagster and Sons, 1851; reprint, Peabody, MA: Hendrickson, 1986), 1061.

[41]Ryrie, *Ryrie Study Bible*, 1489.

[42]Stanley M. Hauerwas, and William H. Willimon, "Your Kingdom Come . . : When We Pray the Lord's Prayer, We Are Relinquishing Our Allegiance to the Kingdoms of this World," *Sojourners* 25 (May—June 1996): 30, 33; Paul S. Minear, *The Kingdom and the Power: An Exposition of the New Testament Gospel* (Philadelphia: Westminster Press, 1950), 31–44, 115–162.

[43]Philip Schaff, *History of the Christian Church*, vol. 1, *Apostolic Christianity: From the Birth of Christ to the Death of St. John, AD 1–100* (Originally published, 1858; reprint, Peabody, MA: Hendrickson, 2002), 472–3.

[44]Gerhard Sauter, *What Dare We Hope: Reconsidering Eschatology* (Harrisburg, PA: Trinity Press, 1999), 203.

[45]John Polkinghorne, *The God of Hope and the End of the World* (New Haven, CT and London: Yale University Press, 2002), 100.

[46]Hauerwas and Willimon, 32–3; Schaff, vol. 1, 466–7.

[47]Larry D. Hart, *Truth Aflame: A Balanced Theology for Evangelicals and Charismatics* (Nashville: Thomas Nelson, 1999), 525; Polkinghorne, 83–4, 101.

[48]Oral Roberts, *Christ in Every Book* (Tulsa: Oral Roberts Evangelistic Association, 1975).

[49]George Eldon Ladd, *A Theology of the New Testament* (Grand Rapids: Eerdmans, 1974), 328–41.

[50]Brent Kinman, "Parousia, Jesus' 'A-Triumphal' Entry, and the Fate of Jerusalem," *Journal of Biblical Literature* 118 (Summer 1999): 288–90, 293–4.

[51]See Ladd, *A Theology of the New Testament*, 550; William J. Dumbrell, *The Search for Order: Biblical Eschatology in Focus* (Grand Rapids: Baker, 1994), 259; M. C. de Boer, "Paul and Apocalyptic Eschatology," in *The Continuum History of Apocalypticism*, ed. Bernard McGinn, John J. Collins, and Stephen J. Stein, 166–194 (New York, London: Continuum, 2003), 191.

[52]See Biederwolf, 412–26, 435–45, 453–8, 461–96, and 498–506; Vincent, 3: 28, 61–2, 65, 85–92, 94–105, 109–447, 120–2, 126–9, 133–53, 165, 168–9, 173, 238–41, 249–53, 266–7, 273–87, and 353–4; 4:115–38; 3:367–76, 381–2, 405–11, 417, and 462–80; 4:19–20, 26–31, 34, 38–58, 62–8, 243–6, 291–4, 298–300, 310–14, 318–24, and 344–6. See also J. Christiaan Beker, *Paul's Apocalyptic Gospel: The Coming Triumph of God* (Philadelphia: Fortress Press, 1982) for more.

[53]Biederwolf, 511–4, 516–20; Vincent, vol. 4, 482–95, 508–39.

[54]Biederwolf, 520–2; Vincent, vol. 1:760–2.

[55]Biederwolf, 522–5, 526–34; Vincent, vol. 1:629–35, 642–4, 658–62, 703–8.

[56]Biederwolf, 541–2; Vincent, vol. 1:719–22.

[57]Biederwolf, 534–8; Vincent, vol. 2:335–44.

[58]Biederwolf, 542–726; Vincent, vol. 2:405–574.

[59]Minear, 31–45.

Chapter 6

[1]Marvin Rosenthal, *The Pre-Wrath Rapture of the Church* (Nashville: Thomas Nelson, 1990), 46.

[2]Timothy P. Weber, *Living in the Shadow of the Second Coming, American Premillennialism 1875–1925* (New York; Oxford, England: Oxford University Press, 1979), 9.

[3]Paul King, "Premillennialism and the Early Church," in *Essays on Premillennialism*, ed. K. Neil Foster and David E. Fessenden (Camp Hill, PA: Christian Publications, 2002), 1, 8–10, 11; Joel Van Hoogen, "Premillennialism and the Alliance Distinctives," in *Essays on Premillennialism*, ed. K. Neil Foster and David E. Fessenden (Camp Hill, PA: Christian Publications, 2002), 120–3.

[4]J. Dwight Pentecost, *Things to Come: A Study in Biblical Eschatology* (Grand Rapids, MI: Dunham, 1958; reprint Zondervan, 1964), 476–7.

[5]Pentecost, *Things to Come*, 482–90.

[6]Pentecost, *Things to Come*, 495–506.

[7]R. A. Torrey, *The Return of the Lord Jesus* (Los Angeles: Grant's Publishing House, 1913), 145.

[8]Weber, 9–11.

[9]Loraine Boettner, "Postmillennialism," in *The Meaning of the Millennium: Four Views*, ed. Robert G. Clouse (Downers Grove, IL: InterVarsity Press, 1977), 117.

[10]Ernest R. Sandeen, *The Roots of Fundamentalism: British and American Millenarianism 1800–1930* (Chicago: Chicago University Press, 1970), 4.

[11]Hans Bietenhard, *The Millennial Hope of the Early Church*, 28–29; quoted in Millard J. Erickson, *A Basic Guide to Eschatology: Making Sense of the Millennium*, 2nd ed. (Grand Rapids, MI: Baker, 1998), 58–9.

[12]Sandeen, 5.

[13]Ed Dobson, Jerry Falwell, and Ed Hindson, eds., *The Fundamental Phenomenon, The Resurgence of Conservative Christianity* (Garden City, NY: Doubleday, 1981), 71.

[14]Columbia Graham Flegg, *Gathered Under Apostles, A Study of the Catholic Apostolic Church* (Oxford, England: Clarendon Press, 1992), 295.

[15]Erickson, 74–75.

[16]King, 1; Van Hoogen, 120.

[17]George Eldon Ladd, *Crucial Questions about the Kingdom of God* (Grand Rapids, MI: Eerdmans, 1952), 23.

[18]Flegg, 295.

[19]Clouse, 9.

[20]Flegg, 296.

[21]Harold Shelly, "Premillennialism in the Medieval and Reformation Times," in *Essays on Premillennialism*, ed. K. Neil Foster and David E. Fessenden (Camp Hill, PA: Christian Publications, 2002), 16–18.

[22]Richard Kyle, *The Last Days Are Here Again: A History of the End Times* (Grand Rapids, MI: Baker, 1998), 49; Shelley, 18–19.

[23]Shelly, 18–27.

[24]Flegg, 297.

[25]Le Roy Edwin Froom, *The Prophetic Faith of our Fathers, The Historical Development of Prophetic Interpretation*, vol. 2, *Pre-Reformation and Reformation Restoration and Second Departure* (Washington, DC: Review and Herald, 1948), 486–90.

[26]Jesse Forest Silver, *The Lord's Return: Seen in History and in Scripture as Premillennial and Imminent*, rev. ed. (New York: Fleming H. Revell, 1914), 118–124, 132–3.

[27]Silver, 134–5.

[28]Robert C. Fuller, *Naming the Antichrist* (New York: Oxford University Press, 1995), 42–3.

[29]Robert Middlekauff, *The Mathers: Three Generations of Puritan Intellectuals, 1596–1728* (New York: Oxford University Press, 1976), 323.

[30]Dobson, Falwell, and Hindson, 71.

[31]Sandeen, 4–5.

[32]Froom, *The Prophetic Faith of Our Fathers, The Historical Development of Prophetic Interpretation*, vol. 3, *Pt. 1, Colonial and Early National American Exposition*; *Pt. 2, Old World Nineteenth Century Advent Awakening* (Washingon, DC: Review and Herald, 1946), 304–5, 309.

[33]Flegg, 40–50.

[34]Sandeen, 29–37.

[35]Sandeen 50–8.

[36]Kyle, 87, who quotes Sandeen, 50.

[37]Kyle, 74.

[38]Sandeen, 82–9.

[39]C. I. Scofield, *The New Scofield Reference Bible* (New York and Oxford: Oxford Press, 1967).

[40]Sandeen, 216–225.

[41]Sandeen, 188–9, 192–3, and 206–7.

[42]Sandeen, 233–9, 246.

[43]Weber, 177–183.

[44]Psalms 2:1–12; 8:4–8; 22:27–31; and 24:7–10; Isaiah 2:1–5; 4:2–6; 9:7; 11:4–12; 32; 35:1–10; 56:6–7; 60; and 66:7–9; Daniel 2:44; Hosea 6:2; Joel 2:28–32; Obadiah 17–21; Micah 5:1–15; see William E. Biederwolf, *The Second Coming Bible Commentary* (Grand Rapids: Baker, 1924; reprint, 1985), 28–30, 30–1, 31, 32, 46, 51–2,

55–7, 58–62, 91–3, 100–02, 109, 112–17, 136–140, 201, 204, 245, 251–2, 261–2, 266–8; and Psalms 95–106; see J. R. Church, *Hidden Prophecies in the Psalms* (Oklahoma City: Prophecy Publications, 1986), 282–301.

[45]Jeremiah 3:14–18; 23:1–8; 29:12–14; 30:1–3; 32:36–44; 50:4–7, 19–20, 33–34; Ezekiel 11:17–21; 28:25–6; 29:21; 34:11–31; 36–37; Hosea 1:10–11; 3:5; 12:9; 13:14; Amos 9:11–15; Micah 2:12–3; 4:1–13; 7:1–20; Zephaniah 3:11–20; Haggai 2:6–9; and Zechariah 8; see Biederwolf, 146–8, 149–52, 153, 153–5, 165–6, 170–1, 172, 180, 181, 182–3, 184–9, 242–3, 245, 246, 259–260, 263, 264–6, 269–70, 273–4, 274–8, and 292–4; and Psalms 48:4–7, 11–13; 51:7; 67; 69:35–6; 73; 84:1–2, 4, 10; and 85:1, 6, 9, 13; see Church, 150–2, 157–8, 183, 201–4, 227– 31, and 231–6.

[46]Herman A. Hoyt, "Dispensational Premillennialism," in *The Meaning of the Millennium: Four Views*, ed. Robert G. Clouse (Downers Grove, IL: InterVarsity Press, 1977), 78–80.

[47]Hoyt, 79.

[48]Hoyt, 80–81.

[49]Hoyt, 81.

[50]Hoyt, 82–83.

Chapter 7

[1]Hilton Sutton, *The Book of Revelation Revealed: Understanding God's Master Plan for the End of the Age* (Tulsa: Harrison House, 1995), 252.

[2]Marvin Rosenthal, *The Pre-Wrath Rapture of the Church* (Nashville: Thomas Nelson, 1990), 118–24.

[3]J. Randall Price, "Old Testament Tribulation Terms," in *When the Trumpet Sounds*, ed. Thomas Ice and Timothy Demy (Eugene, OR: Harvest House, 1995), 82–83.

[4]See David K. Hebert, "The Rapture of the Church: A Doctrine of the Early Church or a Recent Development of the Dispensational Movement?" (M.A. thesis, Oral Roberts University, 2006), 35–36; H. Wayne House, "Apostasia in 2 Thessalonians 2:3: Apostasy or Rapture?," in *When the Trumpet Sounds*, ed. Thomas Ice and Timothy

Demy (Eugene, OR: Harvest House, 1995), 276–277; and Paul D. Feinberg, "2 Thessalonians 2 and the Rapture," in *When the Trumpet Sounds*, 306–308 for more information.

[5]Sutton, 25–27.

[6]Dwight Pentecost, *Things to Come: A Study in Biblical Eschatology* (Findlay, OH: Dunham Publishing., 1958; reprint, Grand Rapids: Zondervan, 1980), 337–338.

[7]Pentecost, *Things to Come*, 337.

[8]Richard Kyle, *The Last Days Are Here Again: A History of the End Times* (Grand Rapids: Baker, 1998), 126–129.

[9]Colin H. Deal, *The Beast and the Arabs* (P. O. Box 455, Rutherford College, NC: Colin H. Deal, 1983); Deal, Revelation of the Beast (P. O. Box 455, Rutherford College, NC: Colin H. Deal, 1995), 9–74; and J. R. Church, *Hidden Prophecies in the Psalms* (Oklahoma City: Prophecy Publications, 1986), 225–226.

[10]Joel Richardson, *The Islamic Antichrist: The Shocking Truth about the Real Nature of the Beast* (Los Angeles: WND Books, 2009), 31–32.

[11]Perry Stone Jr., *Unleashing the Beast: How a Fanatical Islamic Dictator Will Form a Ten-Nation Coalition and Terrorize the World for Forty-Two Months* (Cleveland, TN: Voice of Evangelism, 2003), 185–189.

[12]Deal, *The Beast and the Arabs*; Deal, *Revelation of the Beast* (P. O. Box 455, Rutherford College, NC: Colin H. Deal, 1995), 9–74; Church, 225–226.

[13]Pentecost, *Things to Come*, 326–331.

[14]Pentecost, *Things to Come*, 331.

[15]Pentecost, *Things to Come*, 331–332.

[16]Sutton, 252.

[17]Sutton, 87–96.

[18]Sutton, 102–104, 263.

[19]Sutton, 106–108.

[20]Sutton, 108–111.

[21]Sutton, 113–116.

[22]Sutton, 116–121.

[23]Sutton, 129–136.

[24]Sutton, 195–204.

[25]Sutton, 252.

Chapter 8

[1]See David K. Hebert, "The Rapture of the Church: A Doctrine of the Early Church or a Recent Development of the Dispensational Movement?" (M.A. thesis, Oral Roberts University, 2006), 35–36; H. Wayne House, "Apostasia in 2 Thessalonians 2:3: Apostasy or Rapture?," in *When the Trumpet Sounds*, ed. Thomas Ice and Timothy Demy (Eugene, OR: Harvest House, 1995), 276–277; and Paul D. Feinberg, "2 Thessalonians 2 and the Rapture," in *When the Trumpet Sounds*, 306–308 for more information.

[2]Marvin Rosenthal, *The Pre-Wrath Rapture of the Church* (Nashville: Thomas Nelson, 1990), 53.

[3]George Eldon Ladd, *The Last Things, An Eschatology for Laymen* (Grand Rapids, MI: Eerdmans, 1978), 84.

[4]Spiros Zodhiates, "*harpazo*," *The Complete Word Study Dictionary, New Testament* (Chattanooga, TN: AMG Publishers, 1992), 257.

[5]Hebert, "*The Rapture of the Church*," 13–4.

[6]Zodhiates, "*allasso*," 124.

[7]Zodhiates, "*metatithemi*," 973; J. Lust, E. Eynikel, and K. Hauspie, "*metatithemi*," *A Greek-English Lexicon of the Septuagint*, Part 2 (Stuttgart: Deutsche Bibelgesellschaft, 1996), 301.

[8]Zodhiates, "*metamorphoo*," 968–9. See Hebert, "*The Rapture of the Church*," 14–17, 24–62 for further development of *harpazo* and

other New Testament Greek words similar to *harpazo* used in related passages.

[9]Zodhiates, "*egeiro*"; "*anastasis*," 496, 159.

[10]Hebert, "*The Rapture of the Church*," 19.

[11]John Rea, "The Rapture of the Church and Its Chronological Relation to the Great Tribulation," (M.Th. thesis, Grace Theological Seminary, 1954), 90.

[12]Edward E. Hindson, "The Rapture and the Return: Two Aspects of Christ's Coming," in *When the Trumpet Sounds*, ed. Thomas Ice and Timothy Demy (Eugene, OR: Harvest House Publishers, 1995), 157.

[13]For a full exegetical treatment of the Rapture passages, see chapter 2 of Hebert, "*The Rapture of the Church*."

[14]*The Shepherd of Hermas* 4.1–2 (*ANF* 2:17–18); *The Didache* (*The Teaching of the Twelve Apostles*) 16.3–8, n.14, n.16, n.17 (*ANF* 7:382); Irenaeus, *Against Heresies* 5.5.1; 29.1; 30.4; 31.2; 32.1 (*ANF* 1:530, 558, 560–61); and Victorinus, *Commentary on the Apocalypse* 6.14; 15.1 (*ANF* 7:351, 357); Clement of Rome, *First Epistle to the Corinthians* 23, 24, 34, 35 (*ANF* 1:11, 14); Polycarp, *The Epistle to the Philippians* 2, 5, 6 (*ANF* 1:33–34); *The Epistle of Barnabas* 4, 16, 21 (*ANF* 1:138, 147, 149); Tertullian, *A Treatise on the Soul* 50 (*ANF* 3::231); Cyprian, *Treatises of Cyprian* 7.21, 22, 23, 25 (*ANF* 5:474, –75); and Chrysostom, *Homilies on Ephesians* 3, *Homilies on 1st Thessalonians* 8, and *Homilies on 2nd Thessalonians* 3 (*NPNF* 13:61–62, 356–57, 386).

[15]Randolph O. Yeager, *The Renaissance New Testament*, vol. 15 (Gretna, LA: Pelican Publishing, 1998), 214–16.

[16]George Eldon Ladd, *The Blessed Hope* (Grand Rapids, MI: Eerdmans, 1956), 88.

[17]William Everett Bell Jr., "A Critical Evaluation of the Pretribulation Rapture Doctrine in Christian Eschatology," (Ph. D. diss., New York University, School of Education, 1967), 249.

[18]Hippolytus, *Treatise on Christ and Antichrist* 60, 61, 64, 66 (*ANF* 5:217–219); Cyril, *The Catechetical Lectures of S. Cyril* 15.19 (*NPNF* 7:110).

¹⁹Again, these issues are discussed in greater detail in chapter 2 of Hebert, *"The Rapture of the Church."*

²⁰Rosenthal, 57.

²¹Rosenthal, 60–61.

²²H. Wayne House, "Apostasia in 2 Thessalonians 2:3: Apostasy or Rapture?" in *When the Trumpet Sounds*, ed. Thomas Ice and Timothy Demy (Eugene, OR: Harvest House Publishers, 1995), 276–7; Paul D. Feinberg, "2 Thessalonians 2 and the Rapture," in *When the Trumpet Sounds*, ed. Thomas Ice and Timothy Demy (Eugene, OR: Harvest House Publishers, 1995), 306–8.

²³J. Dwight Pentecost, *Things to Come: A Study in Biblical Eschatology* (Grand Rapids, MI: Zondervan, 1964), 158; Norman L. Geisler, *Systematic Theology in One Volume* (Minneapolis: Bethany House, 2011), 1487.

Chapter 9

¹John Anthony McGuckin, "anthropology," *The Westminster Handbook to Patristic Theology* (Louisville: Westminster John Knox Press, 2004), 13.

²Donald K. McKim, "spirit," *Westminster Dictionary of Theological Terms* (Louisville: Westminster John Knox Press, 1996), 266.

³McKim, "soul," 265.

⁴Alan Cairns, "soul," *Dictionary of Theological Terms*, 3rd ed. (Belfast: Ambassador-Emerald International, 2002), 426.

⁵McKim, "body, mortal," 106.

⁶Millard J. Erickson, *Christian Theology*, 3rd ed. (Grand Rapids, MI: Baker, 2013), 477.

⁷Erickson, *Christian Theology*, 478.

⁸Erickson, *Christian Theology*, 478, 543.

⁹Louis Berkhof, *Systematic Theology* (Grand Rapids, MI: Eerdmans, 1941), 668.

[10]Berkhof, 669–670.

[11]Berkhof, 672.

[12]Berkhof, 675–6.

[13]Berkhof, 675.

[14]Berkhof, 676.

[15]Berkhof, 679.

[16]Berkhof, 675; Norman L. Geisler, *Systematic Theology in One Volume* (Minneapolis: Bethany House, 2011), 1266.

[17]Berkhof, 679; Geisler, *One Volume*, 1218–19.

[18]Berkhof, 680; Geisler, *One Volume*, 1267–71.

[19]Geisler, *One Volume*, 1222–4.

[20]J. Dwight Pentecost, *Things to Come: A Study in Biblical Eschatology* (Grand Rapids, MI: Zondervan, 1964), 219–228.

[21]Geisler, *One Volume*, 1225–6; Pentecost, *Things to Come*, 412–426.

[22]Geisler, *One Volume*, 1266–1274; Pentecost, *Things to Come*, 422–426.

[23]Geisler, *One Volume*, 1247–1250; Pentecost, *Things to Come*, 563–583.

[24]Geisler, *One Volume*, 1301–1316.

[25]Geisler, *One Volume*, 1282–1300.

Chapter 10

[1]William J. Dumbrell, *The Search for Order: Biblical Eschatology in Focus* (Grand Rapids: Baker, 1994), 15–23; See the following: *The Apostolic Fathers, The Letter of Barnabus* 15, trans. Francis X. Glimm, Joseph M. F. Marique, and Gerald G. Walsh (Washington, DC: The Catholic University of America Press, 1962), 4–5; Thomas B. Falls, *The Writings of Saint Justin Martyr, Dialogue with Trypho* 81 (Washington, DC: The Catholic University of America Press,

1948; reprint, 1965); Julius Africanus, *The Extant Writings of Julius Africanus* 3:18:4, in vol. 6 of *The Ante Nicene Fathers (ANF)*, ed. Alexander Roberts and James Donaldson (1886; reprint, Peabody, MA: Hendrickson, 1995); Commodianus, *Instructions of Commodianus* 35, in vol. 4 of *ANF*, ed. Alexander Roberts and James Donaldson (1885; reprint, Peabody, MA: Hendrickson, 1995); Hippolytus; quoted in George Eldon Ladd, The Blessed Hope (Grand Rapids: Eerdmans, 1956), 30–1; Lactantius, *The Divine Institutes*, in vol. 7 of *ANF*, ed. Alexander Roberts and James Donaldson (1886; reprint, Peabody, MA: Hendrickson, 1995), 14, 25.

[2]John J. Butt, *The Greenwood Dictionary of World History* (Westport, CT: Greenwood Press, 2006), 19; *The World Book Encyclopedia* (Chicago: World Book, 2001), vol. 1, 31; vol. 3, 29; Michael J. Radwin, *Hebrew Date Converter*, 2007, http://www.hebcal.com/converter (10 April 2007).

[3]Michael Rood, *Biblical Hebrew Calendar*, 2007, n.p., http://www.michaelrood.com/ hebrew_calendar.htm/ (20 March 2007).

[4]Colin H. Deal, *The Day and Hour Jesus will Return* (P.O. Box 455, Rutherford College, NC: Colin H. Deal, 1981), 124–153; Ann Spangler and Lois Tverberg, *Sitting at the Feet of Rabbi Jesus* (Grand Rapids: Zondervan, 2009), 104–110, 114–124; William E. Biederwolf, *The Second Coming Bible Commentary* (Grand Rapids: Baker, 1924; reprint, 1985), 12.

[5]Jay P. Green Sr., ed. and trans., *The Interlinear Bible; Hebrew-Greek-English*, 2nd ed. (Peabody, MA: Hendrickson, 1986), 691; Butt, 19; *World Book* 2001, 1:31; 3:29; Robert Wilde, "A.D.," *About European History*, 2007, http://european history.about.com/od/referenceencyclopedia/g/glad/ (10 April 2007); Ernest L. Martin, *The Birth of Christ Recalculated*, 2nd ed. (Pasadena, CA: Foundation for Biblical Research, 1980), 1–2, 132–152; H. Wayne House, *Chronological and Background Charts of the New Testament* (Grand Rapids: Zondervan, 1981), 64; Frederick A. Larson, Executive Producer and Presenter, *The Star of Bethlehem Documentary* (Mpower Pictures, 2007); see also, http://www.bethlehemstar.net/; "The Romans Destroy the Temple at Jerusalem, 70 AD," *EyeWitness to History*, 2005, n.p., http://www.eyewitnessto history.com/ (19 June 2015); Hilton Sutton, *The Book of Revelation Revealed: Understanding God's Master Plan for the End of the Age* (Tulsa: Harrison House, 1995), 87–96, 102–104, 263, 106–111, 113–121, 129–136, 195–204, 252.

[6]Deal, *The Day and Hour Jesus will Return*, 92–93.

[7]Joshua J. Mark, "The Hellenistic World: The World of Alexander the Great," *Ancient History Encyclopedia*, 18 January 2012, n.p., https://www.ancient.eu/article/94/.

[8]"The Romans Destroy the Temple at Jerusalem, 70 AD," *EyeWitness to History*, 2005, n.p., http://www.eyewitnesstohis tory.com/ (19 June 2015).

[9]Charles Herbermann and Georg Grupp, "Constantine the Great," *The Catholic Encyclopedia*, vol. 4 (New York: Robert Appleton Company, 1908), n.p., http://www.newadvent.org/cathen/ 04295c.htm/ (19 June 2015).

[10]George T. Dennis, "1054 The East-West Schism," *Christianity Today* 28 (1990), n.p., http://www.christianitytoday.com/ch/1990/issue28/ 2820.html/ (19 June 2015).

[11]Richard Kyle, *The Last Days Are Here Again: A History of the End Times* (Grand Rapids: Baker, 1998), 128–9. Also see chapter 3, Biederwolf, 202–204, 208 and Kyle, 126–129 for further documentation.

[12]Colin Deal *The Beast and the Arabs* (P. O. Box 455, Rutherford College, NC: Colin H. Deal, 1983; Deal, *Revelation of the Beast* (P. O. Box 455, Rutherford College, NC: Colin H. Deal, 1995), 9–74; J. R. Church, *Hidden Prophecies in the Psalms* (Oklahoma City: Prophecy Publications, 1986), 225–6.

[13]"The Roman Empire," *Roman-empire.net*, n.d., n.p., http://www.roman-empire.net/ (19 June 2015).

[14]"The Arab League," *Wikipedia.org*, n.d., n.p., http://en.wikipedia.org/ wiki/Arab_League/ (19 June 2015).

[15]"The Death of Alexander the Great, 323 BC," *EyeWitness to History*, 2008, n.p., http://www.eyewitnesstohistory.com/ (19 May 2015).

[16]Mark, n.p.

[17]Rick Lanser, "Understanding the 2,300 'Evenings and Mornings' of Daniel 8:14," *Associates for Biblical Research*, 30 April 2018, n.p., http://www.biblearchaeology.org/post/2018/04/30/Understanding-

the-2300-e2809cEvenings-and-Morningse2809d-of-
Daniel-814.aspx#Article/ (18 September 2018); Fred P. Miller, "The
2300 Day Prophecy of Daniel 8," Moellerhaus Publishers,
1999–2016, n.p., http://www.moellerhaus.com/2300.htm/ (18
September 2018).

[18] Joel Richardson, *The Islamic Antichrist: The Shocking Truth about
the Real Nature of the Beast* (Los Angeles: WND Books, 2009),
31–32; Perry Stone Jr., *Unleashing the Beast: How a Fanatical
Islamic Dictator Will Form a Ten-Nation Coalition and Terrorize the
World for Forty-Two Months* (Cleveland, TN: Voice of Evangelism,
2003), 185–189; Deal, *The Beast and the Arabs*; Deal, *Revelation of
the Beast* (P. O. Box 455, Rutherford College, NC: Colin H. Deal,
1995), 9–74; Church, 225–226.

[19] Alexander Hislop, *The Two Babylons or The Papal Worship Proved
to be the Worship of Nimrod and his Wife*, 4th ed. (London: S. W.
Partridge, 1929), 5, 50–2, 55; Des Griffin, *Fourth Reich of the Rich*,
rev. ed. (Clackamas, OR: Emissary Publications, 1993), 23–5.

[20] Establishment of Israel: The Declaration of the Establishment of the
State of Israel (May 14, 1948), 6 January 2013,
http://www.jewishvirtuallibrary.org/jsource/History/
Dec_of_Indep.html/ (18 June 2013).

[21] N. W. Hutchings, *The Great Pyramid: Prophecy in Stone*
(Oklahoma City: Hearthstone Publishing, 1996).

[22] This breakdown of the Periods of the Church Age is a compilation
of the following theologians on the matter: J. N. Darby, *Synopsis
of the Books of the Bible*, vol. 3, *Colossians – Revelation*, 2nd ed.
(New York: Loizeaux Brothers, 1950), 561–3; C. I. Scofield, ed.,
The Scofield Reference Bible (New York; Oxford, England: Oxford
Press, 1945), 1332–4; Edmont Hains, *Seven Churches of Revelation*
(Winona Lake, IN, n.d.), 11; Gordon Lindsay, *The Book of Revelation
Made Easy – The Seven Churches of Prophecy* (Dallas: The Voice
of Healing Publishing, 1961), 17–8; Albert Edmund Johnson, *God's
Unveiling of the Future: A Chronological Approach to the Book of
Revelation for Laymen, Bible Students, and Ministers* (1978), 15–6;
and Steve Gregg, ed., *Revelation: Four Views, A Parallel
Commentary* (Nashville: Thomas Nelson, 1997), 62–3.

[23] "Nero Persecutes The Christians, 64 A.D.," *EyeWitness to History*,
2000, n.p., http://www.eyewitnesstohistory.com/ (17 October 2018).

[24]Douglas R. Groothuis, *Unmasking the New Age* (Downers Grove, IL: InterVarsity Press, 1986), 118–120; Ruth A. Tucker, *Another Gospel: Cults, Alternative Religions, and the New Age Movement* (Grand Rapids, MI: Zondervan, 1989), 336–7; Pat Robertson, *The New World Order* (Dallas: Word, 1991), 170–1; "The Coming of Maitreya, the World Teacher," *Shareinternational.org*, 2007, n.p., http://www.shareinternational.org/magazine/old_issues/2007/ s2606_30%20years_small.pdf/ (17 October 2018), Christian Research Institute, "Lord Maitreya," *www.equip.org*, 9 June 2009, n.p., http://www.equip.org/article/lord-maitreya/ (17 October 2018).

[25]"Member States of the Arab League," 14 October 2018, n.p., https://en.wikipedia.org/wiki/Member_states_ of_the_Arab_League/ (17 October 2017).

[26]Joseph Candel, "Signs of the Times: ... And great earthquakes shall be in divers places," *Countdown.org*, 12 March 2015, n.p., https://countdown.org/en/entries/features/signs-times-and-great-earthquakes-shall-be-divers-places/; https://countdown.org/en/signs/ famine-drought/ (17 October 2018).

[27]"Blood Moons," *Timeanddate.com*, n.d., n.p., https://www.timeanddate.com/eclipse/blood-moon.html/ (19 Oct-ober 2018).

[28]"The Deadliest Natural Disasters of 2017," 3 October 2017, n.p., https://www.telegraph.co.uk/education/stem-awards/design/deadliest-natural-disasters/ (19 October 2018).

[29]Lauren Slocum, "The Worst Natural Disasters of 2018," n.d., n.p., https://www.ranker.com/list/worst-natural-disasters-2018/lauren-slocum/ (19 October 2018).

[30]"January 2018 Lunar Eclipse," *Wikipedia.org*, n.d., n.p., https://en.wikipedia.org/wiki/January_2018_lunar_eclipse/ (19 October 2018); Kat Hopps, "Blood moon 2018 date: When is the next blood moon?" 22 June 2018, n.p., https://www.express.co.uk/news/science/ 978316/blood-moon-july-2018-next-eclipse-when-is/ (19 October 2018).

[31]Hilton Sutton, *The Book of Revelation Revealed: Understanding God's Master Plan for the End of the Age* (Tulsa: Harrison House, 1995), 252.

[32]Joshua Project 2007, n.p., https://joshuaproject.net/2007/ (2007).

[33]Wycliffe 2006, https://www.wycliffe.org/2006/ (2006).

[34]Randall Price, "Update on the Building of the Third Temple," *Jewishvoice.org*, 2018, n.p., https://www.jewishvoice.org/read/article/update-building-third-temple/ (22 October 2018).

[35]Adam Eliyahu Berkowitz, "Trump Guided by God's Hand to Help Build Third Temple," *www.breakingisraelnews.com*, 7 December 2017, n.p., https://www.breakingisraelnews.com/99002/trumps-jerusalem-declaration-next-step-third-temple/ (22 October 2018).

[36]Paul N. Benware, *Survey of the Old Testament* (Chicago: Moody, 2004), 137, 142.

[37]J. D. Douglas and Merrill C. Tenney, eds., "temple," *Zondervan Bible Dictionary* (Grand Rapids, MI: Zondervan, 2008), 524.

[38]"The Discovery of the Ark of the Covenant," *CovenantKeepers.co.uk*, n.d., n.p., http://www.CovenantKeepers.co.uk/the discovery of the Ark of the Covenant/ (22 October 2018); Mary Nell Wyatt, "The Ark of the Covenant," Originally published by Ron Wyatt in Fall of 1996 Newsletter, *www.ronwyatt.com*, n.d., n.p., https://www.ronwyatt.com/new_written_account.html/ (22 October 2018).

[39]Chaim Richman, Pre-recorded tour of the Temple Institute, Temple Institute, Jerusalem, 7 January 2019.

[40]Avraham Solomon, "Discussion and PowerPoint on the Ark of the Covenant," Western Wall Administrative Offices, Jerusalem, 8 January 2019.

[41]The Council of The Garden Tomb Association (London), The Garden Tomb (Jerusalem) Association Press Release, "Refuting Ron Wyatt's Claim," n.d.

[42]Richman, n.p.; Solomon, n.p.

[43]Admin, "Exposing The Garden Tomb Association," *Arkfiles.net: Quest for Truth*, January 2018, https://arkfiles.net/?p=398/ (21 January 2019).

[44]Conrad Hackett and David McClendon, "Christians Remain World's Largest Religious Group, But They are Declining in Europe," *Pew Research Center*, 5 April 2017, n.p., http://www.pewresearch.org/fact-

tank/2017/04/05/christians-remain-worlds-largest-religious-group-but-they-are-declining-in-europe/ (17 October 2018).

[45]Ché Ahn, "5 Hot Spots for Global Revival," *Hrockchurch.com*, 17 November 2016, n.p., https://hrockchurch.com/blog/5-hot-spots-for-global-revival/ (17 October 2018); Charles Gardner, "Revival in South Africa – 'Mighty Men' Revival, Linked with Support for Israel," *Openheaven.com*, 26 April 2017, n.p., https://www.openheaven.com/2017/04/26/revival-south-africa-mighty-men-revival-linked-support-israel/ (17 October 2018).

[46]Paul Strand, "Toronto Blessing: 'The Greatest Thing that's Happened in the Church in the Last 100 Years,'" *CBNnews*, 22 June 2018, n.p., http://www1.cbn.com/cbnnews/world/2018/june/toronto-blessing-the-greatest-thing-thats-happened-in-the-church-in-the-last-100-years/ (17 October 2018).

[47]Richard Palmer, "A Religious Revival in Europe?: Feeling threatened by Muslims, Europeans are seeking cultural cohesion in their Christian heritage," *Thetrumpet.com*, November 2017, n.p., https://www.thetrumpet.com/16406-a-religious-revival-in-europe/ (17 October 2018); "'Europe Is Alive for Jesus': Revival Breaks Out in France," *CBNnews.com*, 6 July 2016, n.p., https://www1.cbn.com/cbnnews/cwn/2016/july/europe-is-alive-for-jesus-revival-breaks-out-in-france/ (17 October 2018); Jim Denison, "Is Great Britain Experiencing Revival?" *Charismanews.com*,11 April 2016, n.p., https://www.charismanews.com/opinion/56377-is-great-britain-experiencing-revival/ (17 October 2018).

[48]Oral Roberts, interview by Benny Hinn on *This is Your Day*, 20 August 2004.

CPSIA information can be obtained
at www.ICGtesting.com
Printed in the USA
LVHW080132051220
673227LV00030B/2282

9 781943 489039